PORTRAIT OF EGYPT

PORTRAIT OF EGYPT

LORD KINROSS

WILLIAM MORROW & COMPANY, INC.

NEW YORK 1966

Library of Congress Catalog Card Number 66-26224

Printed in Holland

To
MAGOUCHE

ACKNOWLEDGEMENTS

For the supply of photographs my thanks are due
to Dr. Henry G. Fischer, Curator of Egyptian Art, Metropolitan
Museum of Art, New York, Mrs. Diana Vavasseur James,
Roger Wood, Dimitri and A. F. Kersting.
I must also thank the State Tourist Administration of
the United Arab Republic for their help and courtesy
in the course of a visit to Egypt.

CONTENTS

PART I

Ancient Egypt

PART II

Christian Egypt

PART III

Medieval Egypt

PART IV

Modern Egypt

PART 1 ANCIENT EGYPT

Chapter 1
The River and the Sun

Egypt is, quite simply, a river. "An acquired country," Herodotus called it, "the gift of the river." Welling out of Africa, the Nile flows between its deserts (the "red land") for seven hundred miles, threading on either side of it a ribbon of green cultivation (the "black land") which flares into a delta, like a lotus on the end of a stalk, to fringe the Mediterranean Sea. "Egypt," wrote Amr, the Arab who conquered it, "is a dusty city and a green tree. The Nile traces a line through the midst of it; blessed are its early morning voyages and its travels at eventide."

This long country, tapering southwards, is likewise the gift of the sun. Here the elements of sun and river have compounded to fertilize, to fructify a soil otherwise barren. The sun shines perennially, irrespective of summer and winter. Egypt is a land virtually without rain. When a few drops of it fell in Thebes, just before the time of Herodotus, they were seen as "a strange prodigy". When it falls today in Cairo, a few times a year, it creates bewilderment, causing the people to place newspapers uncomfortably over their heads in default of umbrellas. The Egyptian depends for his nourishment on rains elsewhere.

But the sun is forever with him, visible from morning until evening in a cloud-free, mist-free sky. Its slow undeviating cycle is his life-beat, setting the rhythm of his day. Egypt is a country of the sun. Hence inevitably its ancient inhabitants worshipped, above all other deities — above even the Nile-god — the god of the Sun.

Above the First Cataract, at Aswan, the Nile pours between banks of sand and rock, its ribbon of cultivation wearing away to a thread-bare fringe of palm and thorn. This is the more elemental landscape of Nubia, where in the evening, as the sun goes down, the river hardens from the texture of silk to the texture of steel. The western sky gleams incandescent with an afterglow, first white, then yellow, then palely red, but still alight with the hint of another element below the horizon. There the world turns black.

Towards dawn, a hundred miles farther into Africa, it lightens once more to grey. The glow returns, now to the eastern sky, first red, then yellow, then white as before. Above the western bank there looms, glowing cinnamon in the half light, a rocky bluff from which the façade of a temple emerges — the sun-temple of Abu Simbel. Hewn from the rock, beneath a stylized frieze of apes, sit four colossal effigies of the Pharaoh, giant-footed, mammoth legs dwarfing a retinue of mere mortal offspring. Steadfast and assured — but for one whose head has toppled to the ground — they gaze east across the Nile to face the sun which is about to rise. They face it with certitude, for the architects of the temple so planned and oriented it as to catch the first rays with mathematical precision.[1]

River steamers are moored by the bank, and the passengers, purposeful as churchgoers to early service, file between the knees of the giants into the temple, where they assemble in a nave flanked by eight standing colossi of the godlike Osiris. As the light filters in, they draw apart as though to leave an aisle free for the entry of priest and choir. Instead, like a sudden revelation, it is the sun itself that enters, rising from across the river to pour molten rays horizontally into the temple.

Swiftly they gild the colossi until the nave is bathed in light. More slowly they seep into the sanctuary beyond, then into the ultimate holy of holies, to suffuse the seated figures of four gods carved from stone: two incarnations of the Sun-god — Horus, the morning sun, and Ra the afternoon sun; Ptah, the divine sculptor, who fashioned the world; and the Pharaoh, Ramses II, himself deified as son of the sun. At this apotheosis a hush descends on the congregation — Protestants, Catholics, Moslems, Jews, agnostics all momentarily transformed into sun-worshippers, stirred into reverence at the magic of the rays as at the elevation of a Host.

In the beginning the Sun-god created heaven and earth out of the

---

[1] The temple is now being moved to the crest of the rock, above the level of the floods planned to inundate this stretch of the valley, for the sake of the High Dam at Aswan.

sludge which was chaos. From his mouth he spat out heat and light and moisture; they in turn begat the sky and the earth, with its animal, vegetable, and mineral organisms. Drops of water that fell from his eyes onto his body generated man and woman, notably Osiris, who was to fill a role as the son of God, comparable to Christ's in the Christian hierarchy. The eyes of the divine creator became respectively the sun and the moon.

The setting of the sun to the west of the river, in the white glow of evening, and his rising to the east of it, in the white glow of morning, were explained in terms of a heavenly underworld beneath the flat earth to which his rays, while he cruised through it in a sunboat, brought light by night as they brought it to the sky by day. At his daily resurrection all creatures — even the apes — sang his praises: "Glory to thee, thou who risest in the horizon . . .! Praise to thee: say the assembled gods, 'thou beautiful beloved child.' When he arises mankind lives, and the people exult on his account."

The Pharaoh was his earthly embodiment, the Sun-king claiming divinity — and with it authority not only over Egypt but over the whole of the universe. Each morning, under priestly supervision, he performed ritual ablutions like those of the Sun-god in the ocean of heaven. He thus equipped himself to dispense divine grace to his subjects, for whom the life of the day would not otherwise be thought to have begun. When he died, he "flew away up to heaven and was united with the Sun — and his divine limbs were absorbed into Him who created him." Appropriately, incised in stone on the walls of Abu Simbel, the Pharaoh, trampling his enemies underfoot, flogging and immolating his captives, chaining together his droves of slaves, flaunting his worldly power in its various aspects, portrays himself also in the guise of a man worshipping himself in the guise of a god.

The cult of the Sun-god originated, not here in the south, but in the north, at Heliopolis, now a suburb of Cairo. Here he was worshipped before a sacred stone, pyramidal in shape like a conical diagram of the sun's rays, pouring upon the earth, and with its apex symbolically gilded. From the third millennium onwards the Pharaohs took to building such pyramids on a monumental scale, in the same shape and of ever increasing dimensions, to house and commemorate their own mortal remains.

These pyramids were at Memphis, on the west bank of the Nile, the capital of Lower Egypt, as Thebes was the capital of Upper Egypt: two kingdoms, northern and southern, one with a red crown and one with a white, early united but in perennial rivalry for the mastery of the whole. Today all that remains of Memphis is an eroded alabaster Sphinx with a beard and a contented expression, and nearby a colossus, recumbent still as Herodotus saw it, but caged with a roof over its head, and deprived of its partner, which now towers uncomfortably before the railway station of Cairo.

Palm groves cover the site of the ancient city, reflected in stagnant pools where its fragments lie tumbled — a stone limb on which a wagtail flicks his feathers, the lion's head of a sarcophagus where a lizard lies prone in the sun, the drum of a column with a hiero-glyphic inscription. The setting is the classical Lower Egyptian landscape, laid down in parallel strips — the Nile between high banks, man-controlled; the irrigated fields, crisscrossed by a riddle of ditch-es; the palm plantations, cultivated to a symmetrical rule.

Here harmony between nature and man has achieved an ordered fertility. From the western horizon, where the sun nightly descends into his underworld, the desert takes over, nature consigning the land to sterility. But crowning the first desert ridge, looking back across the living green valley from those cities of the dead where the "dwellers in the west" rest forever, pyramidal tombs punctuate the skyline. Geometrical abstractions of the infinite, these pyramids stands out like man's last defiant assertion of order on the brink of the void.

The earliest pyramid stands at Sakkara, the necropolis of Memphis, which dates from the third millennium before Christ. It was the work of the architect Imhotep, one of the few men of genius whose names have survived from an epoch when artistic creation was largely collec-tive and anonymous. A sage, a physician, and ultimately a god — who was to be taken up by the Greeks, many centuries later, as Aescula-pius, his tomb becoming under their auspices a resort for the cure of cripples — he was, in his capacity as architect, the first man ever to build in stone.

Before his time a man's grave had been covered by a rough heap of stones, like a barrow or cairn, or by a mere heap of sand; then, a little less crudely, by a mastaba, a sloping platform walled with sun-dried brick and palm, designed to protect the grave against raids by jackals. King Zoser, of the Third Dynasty, felt that he deserved some-thing grander, and it was thus that Imhotep, his vizier or prime mi-nister, devised the idea of building him a tomb in stone in place of brick. Bringing loads of fine white limestone from the quarries of Tura across the Nile, he cut and dressed narrow blocks of it and laid them in courses, as though they were bricks, to make walls of them.

Thus he built his first mastaba, covering a pit some ninety feet deep, with a granite sepulchre for the monarch at the bottom of it.

But Imhotep aspired higher than this for the immortal memory of his master. On top of the first mastaba he built in succession another, then a third and a fourth, on a diminishing scale, narrowing almost to a peak, until the tomb was a flight of steps to heaven. It would thus facilitate the ascent of the dead King's soul to the home of his father, the Sun. Gleaming white, this Step Pyramid on the ridge of the Western Desert came to dominate the Nile Valley in the name of its royal and sacred occupant, for many miles around and centuries to come.

Imhotep, an imaginative artist, grew accomplished in the translation into stone of the vegetable motifs of nature familiar in earlier constructions. In the complex of buildings, including other tombs and temples, grouped together in the sacred enclosure, his ceilings are of palm-branches imitated in stone; his columns are of stone "reeds," as though bound together in bundles, their capitals of papyrus flowers or pendant leaves. More curious, in the ceremonial structures designed for the use of the King — or rather, symbolically, for that of his ka, the shadow-self which represented him on earth after his death — Imhotep replaced wooden doors with doors of stone, ever ajar with stone hinges, and wooden palisades, separating the various chapels, with palisades of stone.

Throughout Sakkara, the fountainhead of all stonemasonry, there is an elegant simplicity in the architecture, a refinement in its execution and in the facing of its surfaces. This represents an early flowering of Egyptian art that was never to be repeated, far less bettered, in later dynasties. In the purity of its line and proportions it seems to foreshadow the classical Greek, two thousand years later, and indeed embodies fluted columns suggesting the Doric, but rising to a height of forty feet.

Much was to happen in the millennia between, which did not always reflect an advance in terms of art. First there came a rationalization, a "streamlining" of the form of the pyramid and its aggrandizement to a size which befitted a more powerful dynasty. Some twenty-five pyramids, evolving in various forms and surviving in various stages of repair, string themselves out along this desert ridge, to culminate in the pyramids of Giza, "the mysterious place of the beginning of time". The place is a high white limestone plateau, looking across the valley with its vivid green patchwork of fields and the silvery green fronds of its palm groves to the Nile, gleaming dully, and the desert ridge beyond. It was here that King Cheops, the founder of the Fourth Dynasty, devoted much of his life and fortune to the building of a pyramidal tomb which would surpass those of his forebears in immensity and technical perfection.

The pyramids of Giza, like the skyscrapers of New York, lend themselves to statistical analysis. That of Cheops is four hundred and eighty feet high — nearly half the height of a mountain — and was built, over a period of twenty years, from two million blocks of limestone on a base covering thirteen acres. Many of the blocks weighed two tons or more, and the laying of them called for the labour of a hundred thousand men. At that time, as indeed until less than a century ago, when the annual flood was first controlled, the Nile was for three months of the year a vast lake. The blocks were floated across in flat-bottomed boats, then carried to the site over a long high causeway built for the purpose. The completed pyramid is large enough to contain five of the world's largest cathedrals. Napoleon calculated that there was enough stone in it to build a wall round France.

The burial chamber of Cheops, containing an immense black sarcophagus, is built not beneath the pyramid, as at Sakkara, but in the heart of it. It was air-conditioned by a system of shafts and we approach it, bent double, up a long, narrow ramp. When the body of the King had been entombed, the doors of the chamber were barred by three large slabs like portcullises, and the ramp with sheets of granite, while a special shaft was sunk to enable the last workman to leave it. It was thus hoped — as it proved in vain — to protect it against all depredations. Externally, each side of it was cased in stones, so nicely joined as to convey the illusion of a single slab. But after the Arab conquest they vanished, laying bare a façade of innumerable small steep steps, and thus rendering the summit accessible.

Herodotus makes much of the tyranny of Cheops and his oppression of the slave-labour force that built his pyramid. This version suggests the hostile propaganda of local Greeks, wedded two thousand years later to a democratic system inconceivable in the age of the Pharaohs. In fact his subjects may well have welcomed their employment on such a task during the months of the flood, when no work could be done in the fields. The fellaheen of Egypt were, as they still are, a hard-working people, sun-blessed, gay-spirited, and singing to a rhythmical beat as they worked.

The Greek gossips further assured Herodotus that when Cheops ran out of money he sent his daughter into the brothels with orders to procure him a certain sum. She procured it, but at the same time insisted that each of her clients should make her a present of a stone. With these she built a pyramid for herself, but of noticeably modest dimensions, among others designed for members of the royal family.

Only Chefren, the brother of Cheops, presumed, on inheriting his kingdom, to build for himself a pyramid of comparable size. Like Cheops, he intended to case it with dressed stone, but he died before the work was completed. Its smoth peak, however, survives, shining in the sun like a snow-capped mountaintop. The third pyramid, built by his nephew Menkewre, is less than half the size of the others and points their scale by contrast.

No creation of man, no cathedral or temple or mosque, no tower or skyscraper, no fortress unsupported by any bastion of nature, so dominates a landscape as these three pyramids dominate the valley of the Nile before Cairo. For all their immensity, they are wholly in scale with its long level horizons, and in tone with the changing lights from its measureless skies. One day they stand foursquare and finite, beneath a bright sun, contrasting, in terms of light and shade, those planes which face the four points of the compass. Another day, when the light is diffused, they recede into the distance like a trio of ships, with symmetrical sails, on an ocean; again they seem to float in the sky itself, motionless on a bank of shifting mist like man-made abstractions on the canvas of the heavens. Always they give a focus to the landscape, conveying a hint of some extra dimension.

Modern man is not concerned with the dead men within them nor with the gods whom they worshipped. As pointers to the sun they retain a certain symbolic significance. But to us today their impact is rather that of monuments to the mind of man. They reflect his search for an ordered world nearly three thousand years before our own civilization. They suggest in him a high degree of mathematical science, a capacity for precise calculation and measurement, combined with technical ingenuity and skilled engineering. They display an inventiveness seeking perfection within circumscribed limits. Deprived of all function, the pyramids today have become emblems of pure mathematics, elevated into art for art's sake.

Before the pyramids, protecting the precincts of the dead and the entrance to the underworld, placed where the sun disappears below the western horizon and facing the point at which it will rise once more above the eastern horizon, sits the Sphinx. Hewn from an outcrop of living rock, he is the guardian animal of God and King, a huge recumbent figure of the Sun-god with the body of a lion and the head of the Pharaoh. Between his paws, each fifty feet long, there once stood a dwarfed statue of Chefren, the occupant of the pyramid behind him.

The Sphinx suffered centuries of neglect and maltreatment. A later Pharaoh-to-be, Thutmosis IV, once fell asleep in his shade, at a time when he was buried up to his neck in the sand. The Sphinx took advantage of the occasion to address him in a dream in his capacity as Sun-god:

"My countenance is upon you, and my desire is towards you; and to me you, for your part, shall be a protector, for my present condition is as though I were sick, the sand of this desert whereon I rest having overwhelmed me. Give attention to me, and cause that to be done which I have desired, knowing that you are my son and protector."

In return the Sphinx promised him his kingdom on earth, with power over all the living and the revenues of both Upper and Lower Egypt. On the death of his father Thutmosis was hailed as Pharaoh, to the discomfiture of rival Upper Egyptian claimants, and at once took steps to disengage the Sphinx from the sand. Later, however, the Sphinx silted up again and the stone fell away from his paws and breasts, to be restored by the Ptolemies and Ceasars; later still fanatics tore off his nose and his beard; and in the Middle Ages a Turkish Emir smashed in much of his face by selecting it as a target for musket practice.

Now, disengaged once and for all, he sits battered but unbowed, holding his head high with pride and solemnity and an assurance of benevolent power as he gazes eyeless across the valley and into realms beyond.

The Greeks changed the sex of the Sphinx, making him a lioness. They also changed his character. Their own sphinxes had female heads and breasts, combined with evil feline natures. The riddle of the Sphinx was a Greek, not an Egyptian, riddle. It originated with the sphinx of Boeotia, an ill-disposed goddess with the face of a woman, the feet and tail of a lion, and the wings of a bird, who dwelt on the top of a rocky mountain. She liked to persecute the Thebans with a riddle, devouring them in the event of their failure to guess it. "What is that," she asked, "which is four-footed, three-footed, and two-footed?"

At last Oedipus guessed that it was man — the child who crawls on

Sakkara. Step Pyramid and fluted column of Temple.

Sakkara. Detail of capital.

Giza. The Pyramids seen at dusk across an irrigation canal.

Memphis. Statue of a young Pharaoh at Mit Rahineh, nearby.

Henry G. Fischer

Thebes. The Ramesseum, built as a funerary temple by Ramses II in honour
of the Sun-god and of himself, 'Sun of sovereigns.'

hands and feet, the old man who supports his two feet with a stick, the adult who walks upright. On receiving the correct answer, the Sphinx flung herself down from her mountaintop and troubled the Thebans no more. The Sphinx of Giza, essentially protective to his own people and merciless only to their enemies, posed no such tormenting enigmas.

Chapter 2
The Land and its Gods

The Sun-god, in incarnations which differed from time to time and from place to place — Ra, Amon, Aton, Horus, Khnum — was by no means the only deity whom the ancient Egyptians revered. They were on the contrary a notably polytheistic people. The sun, as the heavenly body most closely affecting the rhythm of their existence, was seen as the main life force in the cosmos, hence the leader of their pantheon. But it was a widespread pantheon, embracing some two thousand other gods besides.

At the head of it, grouped around the Sun, were the various universal deities, impersonal divine essences of the moon, stars, earth, sky, air, dew, the Nile, and the ocean, revealing themselves through natural phenomena. Of similar status were patron gods and goddesses of war, of travellers, artists and craftsmen, of scribes and scholars, law and order, dancing and music, love and joy. Moral, as distinct from social attributes did not figure in this system of heavenly patronage. They were a matter for the civil, not the religious authority, which was of a strictly magical nature.

The Egyptians saw magic in everything around them. The divine spirit, the life force, was in every creature, human and especially animal. Animals, and later animals in human form, played a prominent role in the system of worship. Gods, so the people believed, inhabited the birds and beasts of the Nile Valley, which they worshipped accordingly. As time went on these objects of worship were anthropomorphized, animal heads becoming endowed with human bodies and invested with princely regalia. Thus the Sky-goddess

Hathor, the symbol of womanhood, has the head and ears of the cow, whose four legs were supposed to hold up the heavens. The Sky-god Horus has the head of a falcon, the goddess of war the head of a lioness, the god of the cataracts that of a ram, the Moon-god that of an ibis, a bird revered, according to a traveller's tale of Herodotus, as the killer of a breed of Arabian winged snake.

Birds represented, in principle, the soul, flying away from a man's body at death and perhaps perching in the branches of a tree he had planted, while the mourners lamented his passing. The King, who was not of the earth but of the sky, "goes up to heaven like the hawks, and his feathers are like those of the wild geese. He rushes at heaven like a stork; he kisses heaven like the locust." In predynastic times there were hawk kings, preceded by reed kings, in conflict with hornet kings, while the kings from the First Dynasty onwards were "lords of the vulture and the cobra." Thutmosis III was "a lord of wings who swoops down upon that which he sees."

Numerous animals were sacred, some universally, some regionally. The Fayum, a fertile oasis reclaimed from the marshes to the southwest of Cairo, was the centre of the cult of the crocodile, which haunted its waters and was deified to reign as Sobek, at Crocodilopolis, a city of which only a few scattered ruins survive. In such centres of worship, Herodotus records, the people kept "one crocodile in particular, who is taught to be tame and tractable. They adorn his ears with earrings of molten stone or gold, and put bracelets on his forepaws, giving him daily a set portion of bread, with a certain number of victims; and, after having thus treated him with the greatest possible attention while alive, they embalm him when he dies and bury him in a sacred repository."

The people of Elephantine (Aswan), on the other hand, had so little regard for the crocodile that they ate him. The revered creatures of one region were often thus despised by another. Originally they were individual tribal fetishes, dating back to the times before the Nile was brought under control and the nomadic tribesmen became settled as agriculturalists. Thus, as late as Roman times, the inhabitants of a town of fish-worshippers once raided a neighbouring town of dog-worshippers and, finding them eating a fish-dinner, killed and ate all their dogs.

Dogs, which were protected by Anubis — a god of the underworld with the head of a jackal — were interred after death in the odour of sanctity, their devotees shaving heads and bodies in mourning. So records Herodotus, who adds that, on the death and similar burial

of a cat, its devotees would shave their eyebrows. The cat, as originally worshipped, was an animal as fierce as a lioness, the protector of
men and destroyer of serpents. Later, becoming domesticated, she
was worshipped at Bubastis as Bast, the goddess of joy and the patroness of dancing and music. In her temple she was offered bronze
statuettes of herself by the thousand in human form or otherwise —
feline effigies, pillaged from the site of Bubastis in the nineteenth
century, to find their way, together with innumerable forgeries, to
all parts of the cat-loving world.

Sacred cemeteries abounded, not merely for dogs and cats but for
ibises and crocodiles, all suitably embalmed before burial. The animal
corpses were so numerous that modern generations have used their
remains for the profane purpose of manuring the land. Strangest of
all were the cities of the dead consecrated to bulls, of which an
immense example, the Serapeum, survives at Sakkara.

The bull, whose procreative activities led him to be worshipped
as a symbol of virility and fruitfulness — a fertiliser not only in the
animal but in the vegetable kingdom — was deified as Apis. He
harboured within him the soul of Ptah, the god of Memphis, and was
crowned, between his horns, with the disc of the Sun-god himself.
The divine creature was reborn perennially, his successor selected
from the herd where he was identified by as many as twenty-eight
distinguishing marks on his hide — a white spot on the forehead,
for example, a crescent-shaped mark on the flank, a scarab beneath
the tongue, double hairs in the tail, and on the back, says Herodotus,
the figure of an eagle.

The bull led a pampered life at Sakkara, lying on a luxurious soft
bed in the temple, with his revered mother in a neighbouring stall
and an ample harem of cows within call. Here, in Ptolemaic times
when he was equated with the Greek god Serapis, men consulted
him as an oracle, taking his answer to be favourable if he licked their
hands and foreseeing their doom if he failed to do so.

At his death the bull was treated to a sumptuous funeral, costing
the state the equivalent of many thousands of pounds. The ponderous body of the beast was embalmed with oil, clothed in wrappings
of the finest linen, and adorned with amulets and ornaments of gold
and precious stones. His devotees mourned over him, shaven-
headed, and fasted in his memory, living on nothing but water and
vegetables during the sixty days of his burial ceremonies. Herodotus
alleges that bull's blood was poisonous, and that a draught of it,
administered by orders of the Persian conqueror Cambyses, killed

the Egyptian King Psammetichus. Later, the historian adds, Cambyses made mock of Apis and stabbed him, inflicting a fatal wound on the sacred creature, which earned for the Persian the punishment of permanent insanity.

The bulls were buried deep underground at Sakkara, with numerous offerings and gravestones recording their biographies, their places of origin, the names of their mothers. Here, in a long dark gallery, with cavernous vaults on either side, some two dozen of their monstrous sarcophagi survive, built from huge slabs of basalt or granite. But their lids have been prised away through the centuries to reveal only a macabre vacuum where the holy bulls once lay. Among their worshippers was Alexander the Great, the deliverer of Egypt from the Persians. He had been brought up to think of himself, mystically speaking, as a son of Zeus and the Sun-god, and after his coronation as Pharaoh at Memphis was given confirmation of the relationship by the oracle of the Sun-god in the oasis of Siwa.

Apis, in due time, was dedicated to Osiris, who was supposed, after his death, to have been reborn by passing through the skin of a bull. Thus his cult grew universal. For Osiris was of the family of the Sun-god, and towards the end of the third millennium was to become throughout Egypt more loved, if not more revered, than the Sun-god. For of all the gods in the pantheon Osiris alone is the embodiment, not of a divine abstraction in half-human or half-animal form, but of a complete human being and a human principle in the Egyptian mythology. He became in a sense the equivalent of Adonis in the Greek and of Christ in the Christian religions. For these too endured agony and death and triumphed over it to achieve in their several ways resurrection, giving to the rest of humanity the hope of eternal survival.

The story of Osiris began in the heavens, where he was born of the god of the earth and the goddess of the sky. At his nativity a voice proclaimed that the Lord of All had been born into the world. He subsequently married Isis, his sister. At this period the Egyptians were still cannibals, but Isis discovered wild wheat and barley and Osiris introduced its cultivation, so that the people took to a diet of grain in place of human flesh. He was the first man to take fruit from the trees, to train vines to poles, and to tread the grapes for wine. He was thus one of the founders of civilization, and became justly revered as a god.

But his brother Set grew jealous of Osiris, and with a gang of confederates plotted against him. They made a handsome coffer, and at a drinking party Set promised to present it to the guest whom it should fit exactly. It fitted only Osiris, who had been secretly measured for it beforehand, unawares. No sooner had he climbed into it than the lid was slammed down on him and soldered with molten lead. The coffer was then flung into the Nile. It floated down the river and away out to sea, to be washed ashore at Byblos, on the Syrian coast. Here Isis found it, enclosed in the trunk of a tree which had shot up to protect it, and took it back to Egypt.

Unluckily, Set discovered the coffer and, recognizing the body, tore it into fourteen pieces, which he flung far and wide. Isis took a boat made of papyrus and sailed up and down the marshes of the Delta, retrieving the pieces and burying each limb where she found it. She found all but the genitals, of which she made an image, to be appropriately used by Egyptians in subsequent festivals. So many graves in so many different places caused the cult of Osiris to become widespread, much as the dispersal of the relics of saints stimulates their worship today in a diversity of Christian communities. In the temple at Dendera is an inscription with a list of these graves, while other texts specify the whereabouts of the various divine limbs, including a miraculous multiplicity of legs, and a pair of heads, one at Memphis and one at Abydos.

But eventually, in response to the laments of Isis — comparable to the mythical laments for the Greek Adonis — the Sun-god sent down from heaven the jackal-headed Anubis, the divine embodiment of those wild dogs which roamed through the cemeteries. Anubis pieced the body together, swathed it in bandages, as was customary with the dead, and accorded it the proper funeral rites. Isis then fanned the cold clay of the body with her wings, and Osiris came to life again — to reign henceforward, however, not on the earth but in the underworld, as king of the dead, "the first of the dwellers in the west."

Osiris became the embodiment not merely of power, as his divine associates were, but of goodness and truth, which thus became the prerequisites for eternal life. Henceforward this heaven-beneath-the-earth was open, not merely to a privileged and powerful few as before, but in a democratic spirit and on ethical principles to all mankind whose moral worth was unquestioned. Every dead man was embalmed, as Osiris had been by Anubis, and interred with identical ceremonies to prepare him, like Osiris, for resurrection beyond the grave.

On entering the hall of truth beyond the western horizon, the dead appeared before the great judge Osiris, flanked by a bench of forty-two other judges representing the forty-two provinces of Egypt and the forty-two sins of which they must prove themselves innocent before gaining admission. These covered such general transgressions as lying, slander, fraud, theft, adultery, murder, and — one unfamiliar in the Christian calendar — heart-eating, or useless remorse. With regard to more specific offences the dead would have to declare: "I have not diminished the food in the temples . . . falsified the field measure . . . snared the birds of the gods . . . dammed up running water . . . hindered the god in his revenues." On the contrary, "I have given bread to the hungry, water to the thirsty, clothing to the naked, and a passage over the river to him who hath no boat."

Before his confession, the heart of each candidate for eternity was weighed in the balance by Anubis and Horus to judge whether or not it was lighter than the feather of truth. If he failed to pass the test he was refused admission and consigned to dire punishment and everlasting damnation. Otherwise he embarked upon the delights of eternal life, which closely resembled those of life on earth, but for the fact that the corn grew prodigiously higher and the canals were invariably full.

It became the aspiration of every good Egyptian to be buried at Abydos, in ground hallowed by the buried head of Osiris, and to join his retinue of companions and courtiers in the after-life. Abydos developed into a place a religious pilgrimage like the Ka'aba at Mecca and the Church of the Holy Sepulchre at Jerusalem in a later millennium. The limestone walls of its temple of Sethi I are adorned with reliefs of fine quality and a complete list of the kings of Egypt before his time, a valuable contribution to history. An annual mystery play came to be performed here at Abydos, dramatizing the various episodes of Osiris' life, death, resurrection, and apotheosis among the gods. In this many of the inhabitants and visiting pilgrims took part. Such scenes are carved, in bas-relief, on the walls of the temple at Dendera farther up the Nile. Here the dead god is portrayed on his bier, swathed as a mummy, then rising gradually higher and higher until he leaves it to stand upright between the protective wings of Isis, while a male figure holds before him the Key of Life.

But Osiris was the embodiment not merely of spiritual but of vegetable life in death. In the temple of Isis at Philae, stalks of corn are shown springing from his corpse. For he is also the Corn-god, whose body fertilizes the grain — the god who died that both the spirit and the body of man might live.

Everywhere throughout the countryside Osiris was held to embody the process of vegetation. The harvest was his martyrdom — the severing of his body by the sickle of the reaper and its trampling by the cattle on the threshing floor. His cycle thus represented the rhythm of the seasons. The perennial rising of the Nile was the flood of Isis' tears, mourning her beloved. When it subsided and the seed was sown once more, scattered like the pieces of Osiris' body, an effigy of the god, made of damp clay and corn, was buried in the ground that he might live anew with the new crop. He was also a god of human fertility, represented in ceremonial processions by images which emphasized his reproductive organ. Isis was revered as the faithful wife of Osiris and devoted mother of Horus, to whom she gave miraculous birth after Osiris' resurrection and who avenged his father's death by slaying Set, the incarnation of evil, sterility, and drought, and inherited his father's earthly kingdom. Later images of Isis, suckling him as an infant, form a link with the Christian Madonna and Child.

Thus the grave bearded figure of Osiris abounds throughout Egypt. Swathed in the close-fitting robe of his mummification, wearing the white crown adorned with ostrich plumes, and with a miniature disc of the sun which symbolized his spiritual and temporal power, and holding, crossed over his breast, the sceptre and flail of his rank, his tall slender effigies often serve in perspective as columns upholding the roof of a temple. Everywhere he stands out as a human counterpart to his sterner progenitor, the god of the sun in the form of the Pharaoh.

Chapter 3
The Works of the Pharaohs

The early Egyptians, secure in their long river valley, "walled in" as it were between broad desert wastes, lived in a world of their own. For the first fifteen hundred years of their recorded history they suffered no foreign invasion and attempted no foreign expansion. They were hardly aware of an outside world, but for occasional contacts with the Arab tribesmen who roved through the desert and the negroid peoples who lived above the First Cataract.

Early in the third millennium the predecessor of Cheops made a military excursion into Nubia, on this southernmost frontier, where he found that the river had its source not here, as had been generally supposed, but in remoter African lands many hundreds of miles to the south. In subsequent reigns further expeditions were made to this "Land of Ghosts," extending the Egyptian frontier and returning with loads of incense, ivory, ebony, panther-skins, and various treasures from Ethiopia. From one of them the prize trophy was a dancing pigmy or dwarf, who was accepted as a gift by the boy Pharaoh of the time, with childish enthusiasm and specific injunctions relayed through his mother for his journey down the Nile:

> When he goes aboard the ship with you, appoint trustworthy people who shall remain near him on each side of the vessel; and take care that he does not fall into the water. When he sleeps at night, appoint trustworthy people who shall sleep beside him in his cabin; and make an inspection ten times a night. My Majesty wants to see this pigmy more than all the gifts from the mines of Sinai or from the Land of Incense.

As time went on these peoples of Nubia were seen as a threat to Egyptian security, and the Pharaohs of the early second millennium had fears of a black invasion. They built fortresses in the south, and a great brick wall along the river for the protection of shipping. Finally they invaded the country of the Nubians and secured the Egyptian frontier farther still to the south. A boundary stone was set up, near the present town of Wadi Halfa, "in order to forbid any Negro to pass it by water or by land, either with a ship or with any herds of cattle, forever," except by special permission; while a subsequent inscription showed reassurance at the ease of the conquest. "These Negroes," it read, "are not a brave people after all; they are poor and broken in spirit. My Majesty has seen them, and it is not a lie. I captured their women, I carried off their subjects, I went forth to their wells, destroyed their cattle and reaped their grain or burnt it."

Thus dynasty succeeded dynasty and Pharaoh Pharaoh — three hundred and fifty of them in the thirty-five centuries before Christ — with a continuity unmatched in the history of any other race. The Egyptians lived in blessed isolation and relative peace through the Old and Middle Kingdoms, with their pyramidal societies, their steady economic evolution and their development of the arts and the technical sciences, until the Twelfth Dynasty ended with the succession of a woman to the throne. Disunity followed, numerous Pharaohs succeeding one another in rapid succession to reign over a kingdom now split into two, until in the seventeenth century B.C. the foreigner made his first serious incursion into the valley in the shape of a Semitic horde known as the Hyksos.

Infiltrating from the east, these tribesmen had troubled the Egyptians before with their periodic raids on the Delta, so that a great wall like that of Roman Britain had been built along the edge of the desert, to prevent them from trespassing "even to ask for water for their cattle." But now they came as a more organized fighting force, an unfamiliar black-bearded, hook-nosed race of Jews and Bedouin Arabs who drove chariots into battle drawn by horses, an animal still hardly known to the Egyptians, and wielded with greater efficiency more modern bronze weapons than theirs. They established themselves in the Delta with two successive dynasties of Hyksos, "Shepherd Kings" who reigned as Pharaohs for over a century, making vassals of the Egyptian sovereigns in the south.

But early in the sixteenth century the tide turned. One of these vassals regained some independent control and determined to expel the Semitic intruders — "the Filthy Ones" — with the aid of Negro troops recruited in Nubia. As he recounted:

> I sailed downstream victorious to drive back the Asiatics by the command of Amon. The plans of my army were successful, for every soldier was before me like a flame of fire, and the troops of the Mazoi advanced beyond our lines to search out the Asiatics and to destroy their positions. East and west we were victorious, the army rejoicing at one event after another.

Having defeated the Asiatics, he turned upon an Egyptian prince who had treacherously supported them:

> I spent the night on board my ship, my heart rejoicing, and when the day dawned I pounced on him like a hawk. I overthrew him at the moment when he was cleaning his teeth. I battered down his walls; I slaughtered his people; and I forced his wife to plunge down the bank of the river. My soldiers were like wolves with their prey.

The campaign was finally rounded off by his successor, the sixteen-year-old King Amosis, whose name meant "the moon-child," and who permitted the enemy to march out of Egypt, back across the Sinai Desert to the Judean lands from which they had come. For the Jews this was a foretaste of the Exodus to come; for the Pharaohs it was the start of the New Kingdom, and a great era in which Egypt emerged from her isolation to become a formidable power in the outside world. The succeeding Pharaohs of the Eighteenth Dynasty, aware now that the Semitic races were a force to be reckoned with, built up a strong army and embarked, at the Semites' expense, upon a policy of imperial expansion which was to lead their country through several centuries of glory to an ultimate downfall. This period of conquest was initiated by Thutmosis I who, after subduing the Nubians and so securing his southern Nile frontier, marched triumphantly through Syria to plant a frontier stone on the bank of the Euphrates, six hundred miles to the north.

The capital of Egypt, now reunited, was Thebes, the ancient city whose monuments survive as grandiose ruins, dispersed by the banks of the Nile at Luxor and across the broad Theban plain spreading beyond it. It is a deep-soiled land, bathed in a perennial sunlight which gilds the stubble and burnishes the fresh green crops; a peasant land humming slowly with a chorus of human and animal sounds — the fellaheen crying to the donkeys and the camels which bear them, a child chanting in falsetto discord with the wail of the water-wheel which a bullock draws dumbly in a monotonous circle, while around them a dog barks, a cock crows, doves murmur, sparrows chatter, and the hoot of a river steamer is heard in the distance.

Nature and plant-life were fundamental to the religious beliefs of so earthy a people as the ancient Egyptians, with their deep sense of the miracle of fertility and growth. Vegetable symbolism is at once apparent in the columns of the temple of Luxor, which are bundles of thick papyrus reeds bound together and fashioned in stone. The floors used to become a marsh, when a high Nile flooded the precincts, giving birth to marsh-plants such as are sculpted along the base of the walls of other temples. In its heavy grandeur it provides a foretaste of that imperial architecture which dignifies this land of Upper Egypt.

Its apotheosis is the neighbouring temple — or agglomeration of temples — at Karnak. Within its precincts, sacred to the sun and ten other gods and successive sovereigns, is Egyptian history and theology in stone, symbolized and inscribed in the traditional sequence of pylons, courtyards, pillared halls, shrines, statues, and monuments which grow progressively more massive and imposing as one Pharaonic reign follows another.

Such was the traditional earthly home of the gods, a holy city within a city, endowed with its own lands and revenues, as a monastery is, inhabited by a large staff of priests, scribes, overseers, managers, civil servants, artisans, craftsmen, and other employees of the god. Enclosed within an immense high wall, its stone construction contrasting with the more transitory mud-brick dwellings of the town huddled around it, the temple sought to epitomize and perpetuate the stable elements in an otherwise precarious world, to honour and propitiate the gods, whose forces alone could preserve it from chaos. Unlike the Christian church or the Greek temple, it was a sanctuary for the god and his hierarchy of priests, rather than for the people, who did not worship him publicly and were excluded from the rites in his holy of holies.

The temple of Karnak is approached by an avenue of recumbent sphinxes, each with the arrogant head of a ram, the animal emblem of Amon the Sun-god, and with a Pharaoh in miniature standing erect between its paws. Originally there were a thousand of these mass-produced deities, stretching for a mile and a half along a wide processional avenue, all the way from the temple of Luxor. It was

Thutmosis I, the first conqueror, who in the sixteenth century B. C.
set himself seriously to make of Karnak an architectural monument,
not merely to the heavenly power of the god but to the terrestrial
power of his dynasty. For had he not "set the boundaries of Egypt
as far as the circuit of the sun"? As he boasted, "I have made coura-
geous those who were afraid, for I have banished the menace from
them, and have made Egypt the superior of every land."

To embellish and magnify an earlier temple, he brought limestone
from the quarries of Tura, the source of the pyramids, from which he
built giant pylons, sloping towers, linked by doorways. He brought
also from the First Cataract monoliths of granite which, in his own
honour, he had carved into obelisks to flank these pylons — slim
pointers to the sun which were an elongated and refined form of
the earlier conical stones dedicated to his cult, and which were incised
with appropriate inscriptions. Of these one now survives, seventy-
five feet high but no longer capped as it was with burnished copper.
Successive Pharaohs erected similar monuments, of which one still
stands at Karnak. Others, however, dating from the reign of Thutmosis III, adorn the cities of Rome and Istanbul. Further obelisks of
a similar period stand respectively in Central Park, New York, the
Place de la Concorde in Paris, and (anachronistically named "Cleopatra's Needle") on the Thames Embankment in London. Today
there are probably more monumental Egyptian obelisks abroad than
in Egypt itself.

As reign followed reign and the Nineteenth and Twentieth Dynasties succeeded the Eighteenth, a long line of Pharaohs added
buildings to Karnak, which proclaimed the power and the glory of
the Egyptian Empire in a manner comparable to that of the Roman
emperors in a subsequent millennium. They soon took to recording
their martial triumphs, in Syria and other conquered lands, in bas-
relief on the outside walls, as a counterpart to the sacred scenes
recorded within.

The mightiest of their architectural works — indeed probably the
largest religious building surviving in the world — is the pillared
hall of the temple of Amon, which was built by a series of sovereigns
of the Eighteenth Dynasty, with a skyscraping statue of Ramses II to
guard its doorway. Once again, as with the pyramids, it is the sheer
mathematical dimensions of this hall which give Karnak its initial
impact — 388 feet broad, 170 feet deep, 6000 square yards in area
(large enough to accommodate the whole of Notre Dame in Paris)
with 134 columns in 16 rows, the tallest, with their capitals, 80 feet

high and so broad as to require six men with outstretched arms to
encircle them.

Within the hall a sense of immensity prevails, but also one of
congestion, as in a jungle of giant tropical trees. For the Egyptian
architects were masters of bulk rather than space. The great bulbous
"trunks" of the columns open out at the top into the blooming
flowers or buds of the papyrus plant, their petals supporting a huge
architrave. Here once again is plant-life soaring up towards the
heavens, symbolized by a ceiling on which stars were painted, as the
signs of the zodiac were painted on that of the temple of Dendera.

Today Karnak's columns stand open to the sky itself, which for
all their bulk sets them out of proportion. The huge stone slabs which
roofed the building have fallen, but could well be replaced, restoring
to the temple that scale which is preserved in the later temple of Edfu.
This remains intact, retaining that finite order and symmetry which,
as in a European place of worship, so impressively complements the
abstract mystery of the infinite.

Karnak lacks the refiniment and grace of the temples at Sakkara
and indeed the clean perfection of the pyramids, which date from
earlier, purer times. But in its massive masonry and its imposing
perspectives it is unmistakably a monument befitting an empire.
So also, across the river at the far side of the broad plain of Thebes,
are the mortuary temples of the two "Emperors", Ramses II and
Ramses III. Ramses II, who lived for nearly a hundred years, won
legendary fame from his youth as a great campaigner, married a
quantity of wives and fathered a hundred royal children. His boast
that he had been commander-in-chief of the Egyptian Army since
the age of ten was, most probably, an idle one. But for ten years he
fought wars against the Hittites, a militarist people whose empire,
expanding southwards in the thirteenth century B.C., became a
formidable threat to that of the Egyptians in Syria. Finally, each
power recognizing its match in the other, an offensive and defensive
alliance was concluded between them, and Ramses took the Hittite
King's daughter for a bride.

Peace reigned thereafter, and Ramses, who had a talent for propaganda and a sense of the dramatic, built up his own myth as a divine
conquering hero. In particular he liked to describe and to portray as a
glorious victory the Battle of Kadesh, a crucial but indecisive en-
gagement in which the Egyptians contrived, by a spectacular chariot
charge, to extricate themselves from a trap into which the Hittites had
lured them. As he afterwards told the story, he alone in his two-horse

chariot put two thousand five hundred enemy chariots to flight:

> I dashed at them like the god of war; I massacred them, slaugh-
> tering them where they stood while one shrieked to the other:
> "This is no man, but a mighty god; those are not the deeds of
> man; never has one man thus overcome hundreds of thou-
> sands!" I slew them all; none escaped me . . . . I caused the
> field of Kadesh to be white with corpses, so that one did not
> know where to tread because of their multitude. I fought all
> alone and overcame the foreigners in their millions.

This superhuman exploit is repeatedly and vividly depicted with
the chisel on the walls of his temples, and particularly on those of his
mortuary temple, the Ramesseum or "Mansion of Millions of Years of
the King Usi-ma-Re" (the first name of the divine monarch) together
with other autobiographical scenes of a more ceremonial nature.

The battle-scenes emphasize, for the first time in Egyptian war
sculptures, the human rather than the divine aspect of the warrior, and
thus come vividly to life. No longer above the battle, in the image of
preceding Pharaohs, he is in the thick of it, wielding his weapons at
the reins of a chariot, whose rampant horses trample underfoot an
enemy rabble prone in stylized postures of agony, mutilation, and
death. At Abu Simbel he figures even more vividly on his feet in
hand-to-hand combat, swiftly driving his spear through the body of
a helpless and staggering foe.

The Ramesseum today is a romantic ruin, flesh-pink in the evening
sunlight as the lengthening shadows flood down over the plain from
the ridge of the Theban hills to the west of it. On the ground before
it lies the dark granite head, six feet from ear to ear, of a felled colossus
of Ramses, an enthroned emblem of supreme personal power, which
once towered above the columns of the temple he had built to his own
glorious memory. It surpassed in height the two "colossi of Memnon,"
which sit lofty and aloof on their thrones in the fields nearby.

The Romans identified them as stone images of Memnon, a mythical hero of their own, who fell to Achilles on the field of Troy. When
one of the figures, split by an earthquake, began to emit curious
sounds of vibration with the change in the temperature at dawn, he
was assumed to be calling plaintively to his mother Eos, the goddess
of morning. In fact they are effigies of the Pharaoh Amenhotep III,
a predecessor of Ramses, built for a large mortuary temple, since
destroyed, from a sandstone so fine that the elements have eroded it,

leaving them gigantic but faceless as the abstractions of some contemporary sculptor.

As romantic as the Ramesseum, but more human in feeling, is the
neighbouring mortuary temple of a distinguished successor, Ramses
III, at Medinet Habu. A man of some piety, he too had enemies to
contend with, mainly the Libyans from the west in alliance with the
peoples of the Mediterranean, the roving Greeks, Sicilians, Sar-
dinians, and Philistines from Crete. Having defended his empire
successfully against them, he embarked upon a reign of relative
peace, much of which he devoted to building and to restoring the
buildings of others. "I laid out august parks," he wrote, "full of
flower-gardens and places for walking about, all sorts of date-groves,
sacred avenues of fruit trees brightened with the flowers of every
land, olive groves, vineyards and acres of walled gardens with great
trees along all their many paths." Wine, in his reign, was "as plentiful as water"; lakes were dug for the cultivation of blue lotus-flowers;
trees were planted throughout the country, "so that the people may
dwell in shady places." Ramses III liked to boast of his benevolent rule:

> I made the women of Egypt to go uncovered whithersoever
> they desired, for no strangers nor anyone on the roads molested
> them. I made the troops to live at home in my time, and the
> mercenaries were in their garrisons taking their ease on their
> backs, for they had no fear . . . . Their weapons were put away
> in the store-rooms, while they themselves were full of content
> and happiness, their wives being with them and their children
> around them . . . . I did good to the gods as well as to men, and
> took possession of nothing belonging to other people.

Amid gardens, lakes, and orchards, a labour force of 60,000 built
his temple, which contained "monuments like mountains of alabaster" and statues encased in gold. Its doors were decorated with
electrum and burnished copper, and its altars furnished with vessels
of gold, silver, and copper. Its surviving walls are decorated not
merely with lively and gruesome battle scenes — with the trussing
up, beheading, and maiming of groups of bearded prisoners — but
with scenes of leisure in which he is portrayed as an oriental monarch
(in the Syrian style) among the ladies of his harem, who sing and
play to him, fan him with ostrich plumes, and present him with
bouquets of flowers. Here also are hunting scenes in which animal
and plant life are depicted in a lively, naturalistic style — an antelope
fleeing from the royal spear, a wounded bull charging through reeds

Thebes. Head from a granite colossus of Ramses II, fallen to the ground in the Ramesseum.

Above: Nile Delta. Head carved on a sarcophagus of the New Kingdom at Tanis.

Below: Abu Simbel. Façade of the rock-cut Temple of the goddess Hathor and Queen Nefertari.

to its death by a stream in which fish swim regardless. The successive gateways and courtyards of the temple form a symmetrical perspective looking eastwards over the luminous, fruitful fields of the plain and westwards to the barren hills, glowing with the rose-coloured radiance of sunset.

Faced with these various Pharaonic monuments, the eye has to dissociate itself from any conception of classical proportions. But to this there is a single exception, the temple of Hatshepsut, a female Pharaoh who reigned early in the New Kingdom just before the great age of imperialist expansion and architectural ostentation. Here by contrast is architecture in which the principle of beauty seems to override that of power. The temple, built not in the plain but under the lee of the Theban hills, at Deir el Bahri, mounts in three long terraces, linked by a causeway, to the base of a towering cliffside. It is a fine choice of site, in which the rock-face, ravaged and serrated by the forces of nature, looks down dramatically upon the serene colonnades of the man-made temple set symmetrically beneath it. In its style and proportions are a grace and simplicity foreshadowing those of the Greek temples to come a thousand years later, while its fluted polygonal columns were such as the Greeks were to devise and perfect for themselves in the Doric.

The temple of Hatshepsut, like that of Sakkara fifteen hundred years earlier — and unlike those of the more standardized era which followed — bears the stamp of the work of a single artist; and indeed its design and construction were largely inspired by one Senmut, the Queen's favourite, who built for her as Imhotep had built for King Zoser. Senmut, "who entered the palace in love and came forth in favour," dominated her court and effectively held in subjection her young nephew, Thutmosis III, to whom she was Queen Consort as she had been to his father. With his aid and that of the nobles around him, she was eventually proclaimed Pharaoh in her own right, claiming divine origin as sovereign of the hawk, reed, hornet, vulture, and cobra; designating herself King, not Queen, and insisting on her address in the masculine, not the feminine gender; portraying herself, on the walls of her temple, in the form of a man, in male attire with a god's headdress and a beard on her chin. These portraits were to be ruthlessly excised from the walls of the temple by Thutmosis III when she ultimately died (perhaps murdered by enemies or former friends) and he came into his lawful inheritance.

Hatshepsut, meanwhile, was no Amazon, no masculine warrior. She devoted her reign rather to the arts of peace. She despatched a costly expedition down the Red Sea to the land of Punt, probably in the region of the modern Somaliland, which returned with incense trees to plant in the temple precincts and five shiploads of gold, silver, antimony, ivory, ebony, semi-precious stones, ostrich feathers, panther skins, boomerangs, and other such exotic products, together with live giraffes, panthers, baboons, and other breeds of monkey. This profitable venture is nicely depicted in bas-relief on the walls of a colonnade of the temple, where the dusky potentates of Punt and their slaves pay appropriate homage to the powerful Egyptian Queen. Their treasures were presented to Amon, to whom the temple was dedicated, at a ceremony for which

> she herself with her own hands perfumed all her body with the best of the incense, so that her fragrance was like the breath of God, and her scent was mingled with that of the land of Punt; and her skin was decorated with white gold, shining as do the stars in the canopy of heaven in view of the whole land.

Appropriately a shrine in the temple was dedicated to Hathor, the great lady of the heavens and wife of the Sun-god, who was revered as the patroness of the female sex. She took the form of that cow which supported the heavens and nursed those on earth. Hatshepsut drinks from the cow's udder on the walls of the shrine, whose capitals are carved into the likeness of the animal's head — a head which, in later dynasties, became that of a woman with a cow's ears or horns. Here its gentle placid expression helps to enhance that atmosphere of feminine refinement which sets Hatshepsut's mortuary temple apart in this otherwise masculine Theban necropolis.

Chapter 4
The Cult of the Dead

Queen Hatshepsut excavated for herself a tomb in the heart of the cliff behind the temple, approached from its opposite face by a tunnel one hundred feet long. It was here, in a wild and remote canyon, that the Pharaohs of the New Kingdom chose to be buried — beyond, as it were, the western rim of the world and on the fringe of the underworld. Pyramids, they had realized, were too conspicuous, hence too easily robbed of the treasures within them. Thus, instead of proclaiming their tombs to the skies, they tunnelled deep underground to conceal them from covetous eyes.

Thutmosis I, the Queen's father, was the first to adopt this place of burial, choosing a secret site beneath a precipitous slope at the head of the canyon. Here his architect arranged for the hewing of the rock-tomb for "His Majesty alone, no one seeing, no one hearing," whose situation his mourners swore not to reveal. Hatshepsut had his body removed and re-buried in her own tomb at the opposite end of the canyon, so that they should be together through eternity. Nevertheless, in the nineteenth century A.D. only their empty sarcophagi were found in the tomb.

This Valley of the Tombs of the Kings, as it came to be called, is an underground necropolis of deep narrow tunnels and precipitous stairways leading down to some sixty burial chambers, squarely hewn from the recesses of the rock. Dark, claustrophobic, and often so stifling that the air of the outside world, by comparison, strikes the nostrils with a sharp smell of ozone, they impress primarily as feats of subterranean engineering. Here the mummified Pharaohs lay buried

in mammoth sarcophagi, surrounded by such amenities and com-
forts as to enable them to live in heaven in that style to which they
had been accustomed on earth.

First the body was mummified, to preserve the form it had in life
and to ensure its physical resurrection, or at least that of its spiritual
counterpart, the ka — an immaterial self which was still linked with
it and itself needed material sustenance. At first only the rich could
afford the expense of embalming with ointments and spices, dehy-
dration with soda and bandaging with linen steeped in gum, which
the process of mummification involved. As time went on the art
developed to the point at which the mummies became all sinew and
bone, with barely a covering of skin. The internal organs were
removed and preserved, lest they cause the corpse disagreeable sen-
sations, in "Canopic" jars of alabaster or earthenware. But the heart,
since it had to be weighed against Truth by the responsible goddess,
was replaced in the body. Under the New Kingdom the process
became so thorough that every finger and toe was separately band-
aged.

Herodotus at a later date describes three mummification processes
at differing rates of expense. For the rich:

> The embalmers take first a crooked piece of iron, and with it
> draw out the brain through the nostrils, thus getting rid of a
> portion, while the skull is cleared of the rest by rinsing with
> drugs: next they make a cut along the flank with a sharp Ethio-
> pian stone, and take out the whole contents of the abdomen,
> which they then cleanse, washing it thoroughly with palm wine,
> and again frequently with an infusion of pounded aromatics.
> After this they fill the cavity with the purest bruised myrrh,
> with cassia, and every other sort of spicery except frankincense,
> and sew up the opening. Then the body is placed in natron[1] for
> seventy days, and covered entirely over.

Those of more modest means were embalmed by an injection of
cedar-oil, which liquified the intestines and stomach. The poor had
to be content with a cheaper process of evisceration, preparatory
perhaps to being left out to dry in the sun. In later times a dip of
mumiya, otherwise bitumen, was used instead of the soda, giving
rise to the word "mummy," while such monarchs as Alexander the
Great were preserved in honey.

---

[1] Sodium carbonate, used to dehydrate the tissues.

A number of mummies survive in the National Museum in Cairo to give us an impression of these Pharaohs and their Queens as they looked in life. A short race of men, slim and wiry in build with long noses, high cheekbones, and pointed chins, they alternate between the robust and the more effeminate type. Thutmosis II, who was dominated by his consort, Queen Hatshepsut, looks gentle and weak where he lies with his arms crossed over his chest like Osiris, his fingernails manicured and his hair artificially waved. But his son, Thutmosis III, who finally succeeded Hatshepsut and reasserted his authority, looks strong and energetic, with a wide smiling mouth and an authoritative beak of a nose.

His grandson, on the other hand, Thutmosis IV, is once more the delicate type, with slender hands, a good-looking face, and ears pierced for earrings. Hatshepsut's mother, the wife of Thutmosis I, has her hair dyed red and plaited with false locks of black, while the decayed state of her teeth suggests that she must have endured agonies from toothache. Most impressive of all is Ramses II, tall and gaunt and grey-headed and still handsome after a reign of nearly seventy years, with full lips, a hooked nose, bushy eyebrows, and a look of authority still on his face. When these royal mummies were removed by boat from Luxor to Cairo in 1881 the fellaheen, long in memory, mourned them as at a contemporary funeral, the women wailing and tearing their hair, while the men fired salvoes into the sky.

According to Pharaonic practice, when the mummy was ready for burial it was conveyed to the tomb. Here it was stood upright while the family mourners bade it farewell. Then in a ritual ceremony, involving the sprinkling of water and burning of incense, its mouth was opened by the priest with a chisel of metal or flint. This restored the natural bodily functions, as those of Osiris had been restored by Isis and Horus. An assortment of food and drink was then served to the mummy, for miraculous consumption, while the relatives consumed with it some of the divine essence of their ancestors.

After the mummy had been placed in the coffin — which, in the New Kingdom, was shaped to its form and likeness — and the coffin placed in the sealed sarcophagus, meat and drink, fruit, flowers, and ointments were regularly provided for the refreshment of its spiritual self, who emerged through a false door to collect them. But eventually the jars which contained the intestines were held to supply adequate nourishment through their magical powers, supplemented perhaps by models in clay or in wood, of geese and other such foodstuffs. Less directly the recitation of sacred formulas inscribed in the tombs would bring the necessary provisions.

A variety of furniture and other objects, growing more luxurious as time went by, was entombed with the dead man to serve his needs in the afterlife. There might be knives for hunting and self-defence, a chessboard for recreation, hair ornaments and mirrors to assist his toilet, a clay boat to facilitate his transport on the rivers and lakes of the underworld, even a model house in which to live. Small human figures modelled in clay provided him with farm labour or domestic service, filling granaries, of which he was supplied with models, grinding corn for him between stones, making bread of it and brewing it into beer. Above all he had women, whether naked or clothed, lying in his bier or crouching beside it, to gratify his amorous desires.

Meanwhile, his body had been adorned with a quantity of amulets in gold and precious stones — sceptres, crowns, eyes, models, and symbols of the gods. Most significant of all was a scarab-beetle, the emblem of the Sun-god, placed over the heart, so that when weighed at the last judgment it should not be found wanting. A final offering would be a statue of the dead man, placed as a rule in an adjoining chamber where he could be within sight of his worshippers and within earshot of the priestly recitations.

The tombs in the Valley of the Kings grew larger and the burial chambers were hewn deeper into the mountain, as time went on and the wealth of the expanding New Kingdom increased. Every inch of their wall-space is covered with paintings — and occasional shallow reliefs — which bear more relation to scripture than to art as such. They are, for the most part, transcribed wholly or partly in hieroglyphics, and illustrated in conventional pictorial form with the sacred figures to which they refer. Rigidly traditional in design, repeating each other as from a stereotype, flatly rendered on stucco in two dimensions, they resemble a sequence of theological cartoons — an impression intensified in a chamber of one of the tombs, that of Sethi I where, unfinished and uncoloured, they are simply black-and-white drawings in outline.

The religious works from which the scenes and inscriptions are taken include the *Book of Him Who Is in the Underworld*, describing in twelve chapters a land divided into twelve regions or caverns, which correspond to the twelve hours of night, and to which the Sun-god, travelling through the underworld in his boat, brings a brief spell of light; the *Book of Gates*, describing the twelve gates or pylons, guarded by snakes, which lead from one region to another; *The Sun's Journey in the Underworld*, which describes it further; *The Praising of Ra*, a long hymn to him; *The Opening of the Mouth*, describing the funeral ceremonies and other mythological events. The intention was to illustrate, in microcosm and in two dimensions, the world which the dead Pharaoh was now to enter, after his last judgment, and to portray him living among its gods and other inhabitants. To the uninitiated it is a bewildering series of geometrical abstractions and symbols, of sacred objects and places and ceremonies, of deities with human and animal heads, demons, spirits, and other denizens of an unfamiliar and fabulous universe.

Very different from these tombs in the secluded royal valley are the more private "Tombs of the Nobles," the officials and courtiers of the Pharaohs. These informal places of burial were hewn from the eastern face of the rock at el Kurna, looking down from the world of the dead over the plain to the Nile and the world of the living beyond.

On their walls is depicted the life of the actual world rather than the life of the underworld. Freedom of artistic expression breaks out from the bonds of ritualistic convention to portray, still in the flat but with sensitivity, and often with wit, the living Egyptian and his domestic activities. The "cartoons," as it were, come alive.

So creative a spirit first flowered a thousand years earlier, in the Golden Age of the Old Kingdom at Sakkara, when Memphis was capital, and, as here, in the tombs not of kings but of officials. At Sakkara the medium is a fine low relief, from which the painted figures stand out, as those at Thebes do not, with the light and shade of a third dimension. In a sequence of everyday scenes, men, women, beasts, birds, fishes, and plants are modelled with accuracy and a loving attention to detail. Oxen, stylized in herds, or singled out individually for their circumspect, bovine expressions, are driven home from the fields by a file of lithe dark herdsmen. Teams of them draw the plough, while in a lower register rams with horizontal twirling horns trample the seed into the earth, and at a later stage reapers raise their sickles to cut the ripened grain.

Hunters skim in boats through the marshes to harpoon open-mouthed hippopotami, one of them snapping its jaws on a crocodile. Around them locusts and frogs lurk in the reeds, kingfishers flutter over a nest of their young, cranes and hoopoes perch decoratively among the papyrus flowers, stalked warily by predatory cats which were used for hunting in the papyrus thickets. Scribes add up accounts and keep inventories in their master's estate office. High-kicking acrobats dance before him to the rhythmical clapping of slim naked maidens. These are records of life, elevated to works of art by a sense of movement, a delight in the visual patterns of work and of play, a tender eye for the charms and oddities of nature.

The second free flowering of Egyptian mural art belonged to this later Golden Age of the New Kingdom at Thebes. While the tombs of the Kings represented the world into which they were proceeding, those of the nobles represented rather the world in which they had lived on earth. Here are their own homes, their own estates, their own wives and children, servants and farmworkers—and themselves represented more often in a personal portrait than as a conventional symbol. Here, not as a rule sculpted in relief but painted in fresh colour, on light stuccoed walls, with imagination and human perception and an easy fluidity of line, is the way of living, growing more gracious with growth of the Empire, of a well-to-do Egyptian family. The paintings reflect above all enjoyment of life, of the fruits of the earth and of the civilized pleasures in which its landed proprietors liked to indulge.

They were, it is clear from these murals, fond of dancing, or at least of watching it, lissom slave girls or professionals performing before them with sinuous ripples and contortions of their naked limbs. They were fond of music, employing orchestras with players of both sexes. The stringed instruments were the harp, large or small, and a lute like a mandolin; the woodwinds were the flute, single-piped or double, and a nasal instrument like the oboe; the brass was a trumpet which emitted a mournful note; the percussion instruments were drums, tambourines, and castanets, and the hand-clap, beating out a primitive rhythm. A familiar figure among the musicians was a blind singer or harpist.

Such entertainments figure often in pictures of banquets, at once formal and gay in their atmosphere. Host and hostess preside over the guests, gentlemen on one side, ladies on the other, receiving offerings of necklaces and bouquets from servant girls. In one painting a girl pours a drink into the cupped hands of a lady. In another a male guest, who has drunk too freely, vomits discreetly into a bucket with the aid of a friend.

Wine provided constant refreshment. The annual vintage is a favourite theme for illustration: the grapes picked and dropped into baskets, then trodden out in a tank under the feet of the workers in the vineyard; the ensuing liquid in due time poured into jars which are counted and recorded by a scribe on a tablet. In one tomb, that of Sennufer, a mayor of Thebes, the whole of the ceiling, left purposely rough, has been painted with a grapevine rich in fruit, doubtless reproducing the arbour in which the mayor in his lifetime liked to relax and to relish the *douceur de vivre* of his age.

In the tomb of Userhet, a royal scribe, a barber is at work in the open air. His clients are depicted with lively humour as they sit having their heads shaved, or squatting around, laughing and gesticulating and talking as they wait their turn. On a wall of the tomb of Djeserkarasonb a lady sits on a low chair at her toilet. Two naked slave-girls wait on her, straightening a lock of her plaited black hair, holding out for her a lotus and a necklace of flower-shaped beads. The lady's hand-mirror would be of polished bronze, her dressing-table furnished with alabaster jars and glass bottles containing her various powders and creams. Her costume, in the balmy climate of ancient Egypt, was light, consisting mainly of a long transparant pleated robe of fine linen, with a shift underneath and sandals of papyrus on her well-pedicured feet. She rouged her cheeks, reddened her lips, darkened her eyelashes, dyed her hair, and wore a profusion of jewelled necklaces, bracelets, rings, and brooches.

Men, in public, wore a similar robe over the loincloth which was their normal attire. They shaved with metal razors. Neither men nor women wore hats, a practice to which Herodotus ascribed the hardness of Egyptian heads. But on social occasions both donned elaborate perfumed wigs and displayed a fancy for floral garlands.

The ancient Egyptians were keen sportsmen. The Pharaohs, armed with bows and copper arrows, hunted from chariots drawn by "horses swifter than the wind." Amenhotep III boasts in an inscription of how, as a boy of thirteen, he led a roundup of wild cattle, which were driven down a valley into a wall of rope-nets and there, helplessly entangled, shot down to the number of a hundred-and-seventy head. Of these the young Pharaoh accounted for fifty-six, shooting twenty more four days later. During the first decade of his reign he was reputed to have killed a hundred-and-two lions, an average of more than ten per year, while on foreign expeditions he recorded victories against the Syrian wild asses, the elephants of the Orontes, and a rhinoceros encountered by chance in the Sudan.

Smaller game were pursued by all, largely for the pot. The peasants caught antelopes and gazelles in traps or lassoed them, then fattened them up in captivity. These animals figure gracefully in the paintings of the tombs, notably one draped around the neck of a boy, as lambs or kids are draped in archaic Greek sculpture. Userhet had himself portrayed in his tomb as a hunter pursuing a drove of antelopes and hyenas. A hare, sketched on the wall with a freedom and facility which convey his frantic speed, leaps forward from beneath the bellies of his horses to escape the hunters, while a fox crouches frightened and dying, with bloodshot eye, beneath a neighbouring bush.

Wild-fowling and fishing were general sports. In the tomb of Menna, the hunter in his boat aims his weapon, a curved throwing-stick, at a flight of duck, which take off in a flurry, with stylized out-stretched wings, from the papyrus thicket, leaving the hens to mind the nests. At the same time one of his companions in another boat strikes his harpoon into a draught of brightly coloured fishes. Offerings of produce from Menna's estate, fish and fowl, grapes and figs, jars of wine, eggs and dishes of food, form a nicely composed "still-life" on his walls. Elsewhere he makes a pictorial survey of the cycle of cultivation, from ploughing through sowing and harvesting to threshing, on the land for which, as steward and estate inspector to the Pharaoh, he is responsible. The land surveyors record its fruits and the revenue officials assess the taxation. For all its hardheaded monetary overtones, this is a pastoral idyll fit for Arcadia.

Funeral and other ceremonies figure on the walls of the tombs, but as essentially human and personal occasions. A procession with the dead and mummified couple, Menna and his wife, by boat to the sacred shrine of Osiris at Abydos becomes a family excursion down the Nile. The mourners at the funerals, paid for the task as they may be, seem genuinely to mourn, bowing heads and beating brows in a semblance of controlled but heartfelt grief.

Other funeral scenes show the outlandish foreigners who brought tribute to the Pharaohs. Rekhmire, a Grand Vizier of Thutmosis III, displays in his tomb no fewer than three hundred square yards of mural paintings, of which the most picturesque shows his reception of Abyssinians, Cretans and Aegean islanders, Nubians, Syrians, and "People of the South," bringing the usual offerings of vases, chariots, skins, precious stones, and wild animals, including a giraffe and a bear.

The workmen who built these tombs and performed other funeral tasks in the Theban necropolis lived in a neighbouring village of their own at Deir el Medina, building their houses on one side of the street and their own tombs on the other, and decorating their walls with scenes which have much of the naïve directness of prim-itive painting. Thus ritual ceremonies become homely scenes and the animal-headed gods have the charm of domestic pets.

Chapter 5
Akhnaton and Tutankhamen

In the middle of the fifteenth century B.C. the continuity of the New Kingdom was interrupted by a sharp break with tradition. Religious in its essence, it was the work of Amenhotep IV, who sought to replace the many gods of his people with one god alone. The divinity of his choice was Aton, an incarnation of the Sun-god, already familiar at Heliopolis as representing his visible disk. He was now to replace Amon, a god rather of the sky and of fertility, who had reigned supreme in the firmament as the natural divinity of Thebes since the expulsion of the Hyksos. Amenhotep dropped from his name the divine prefix of Amen (Amon) and became known as Akhnaton. Later he was to erase from the walls of the temples all representations of Amon.

Akhnaton was a youthful heretic, a good-looking boy of sixteen with refined features, delicate health, and a nervous disposition. A tendency to dream reflected a mystical spirit, involving positive beliefs and an obstinate determination to realize them. In taking this stand he was deliberately challenging the vested interests of a priesthood, dedicated to Amon, which had been consolidating its power as the centuries went by. Already, on his accession at the age of thirteen, he had discomfited the priests by vesting in the Crown the office of solar High Priest, thus reverting to a practice of the Old Kingdom. The priests, still insisting on the worship of Amon, now made life so uncomfortable for Akhnaton that he mobilized eighty thousand of his followers and left Thebes to establish his capital at Tell el Amarna, halfway down the Nile in the direction of Memphis.

He chose this site because it was virgin soil, hitherto untainted by any religious affiliations. Henceforward it was to become the "Horizon of Aton."

Building swiftly, he made of it a city "great in loveliness, delighting the eyes with her beauty." His palace, built amid gardens, with fine mural paintings and painted floors, outshone in elegance his parental home at Thebes. Here he lived with his pretty wife, Nefertiti, "the lady of happiness, full of grace," and a quantity of daughters, surrounded by the tasteful homes of his nobility. The city was laid out with broad streets and parks, adorned with kiosks, pavilions, and ornamental lakes with islands reached by graceful bridges. A fine temple was erected to Aton, on the lines of the ancient sun-temple of Heliopolis, with smaller temples around it.

Akhnaton, a thousand years before his time, saw his god as a single intangible spiritual essence, embodying absolute good, truth, love, and happiness. The loving father and mother of all mankind, Aton was yet without human form, hence not to be represented in sculpture or painting. He manifested himself through the rays of the sun, whose energy was the life force on earth, creating art, love, laughter, health, the fruits of nature, food, drink, and beauty — "the singing of the birds, the sound of the wind, the ripple of water." Akhnaton apostrophized him in a long hymn of praise, comparable to the Psalms of the Bible:

> Thou appearest resplendent on the horizon of the heavens, thou living sun, who wast the first to live. Thou arisest on the eastern horizon and fillest the earth with thy beauty. Thou art beautiful and great, radiant, high above the earth. Thy beams encompass the lands, all thou hast created . . . . The inhabitants of Egypt are joyous; they awake and stand upon their feet when thou hast raised thyself. They wash their bodies and lay hold on their garments. They raise their hands and extol thee. The whole land sets to its work. All the flocks are content in their pastures. The trees and herbs become green, the birds flutter in their nests, and lift their wings to praise thee. All creatures leap upon their feet; all that flutter and fly, live when thou arisest for them.

In this spirit Akhnaton evolved a concept of art as revolutionary as his concept of religion. It must sweep away all the old traditions, portray humanity and nature, no longer in academic conventional terms but as they were in reality. Every man must learn to see the world through his own eyes, as the simpler folk saw it already. The artist must forsake the stereotype to express his own individual vision. Thus portrait sculpture became the fashion, aspiring to represent living, breathing human beings, carrying realism often to the point of distortion and almost of caricature.

This is exemplified especially in the statues and bas-reliefs of Akhnaton himself, with his heavy-lidded eyes, thick lips, elongated chin, and androgynous figure, with narrow waist, broad hips, and rounded belly — features so exaggerated as though to mock, with a suggestion of decadence, the orthodox effigies of previous Pharaohs. In pursuit of artistic truth, Nefertiti is portrayed as the classic Egyptian beauty, but with a cataract in one eye, and in later years as a modern artist might have modelled her, less fragile, heavier in features, but with a stronger and more forceful head.

Elsewhere they are shown together as a happy domestic couple, embracing one another or sharing a meal, while in more formal reliefs, seated beneath the stylized rays of the Sun-god, they become devoted parents, fondling and playing with their children. On the walls of Akhnaton's palace the beauties of nature — especially of the natural plant forms — were portrayed as accurately and sensitively as in any pre-Raphaelite painting, and with a greater refinement than in the murals of the Tombs of the Nobles. Moreover, the painter's art takes a step forward in a portrait of two small princesses with strange elongated heads, painted no longer in the flat but in the round, with light and shade to give relief.

But none of this was to last. For Akhnaton was not only a mystic and an artist but — once again born into the wrong millennium — a pacifist. It was his idealistic but vain aspiration to achieve political unity within both his African and his Asiatic dominions, through a common religion, the worship of Aton. Thanks to the Sun-god's beneficent rays, love and happiness and everlasting peace would descend upon all his people, at home and abroad.

Unluckily his world was not ready for so radical a metamorphosis. The enemies of Egypt in Syria marched against her friends, who sent frantic appeals to Akhnaton for support — but in vain. As city after city was lost, the inhabitants of one of them lamented, "Thy city weeps, and her tears are flowing, and there is no help for us. For years we have been sending to our Lord, the King of Egypt, but there has come to us not a word, no, not one." "If no troops come in this year," wrote another, "the whole territory of my Lord the King will perish."

And so it did. While Akhnaton sat in Tell el Armarna, performing his religious devotions, preaching love to his people, practising the arts of peace and civilization, his empire crumbled to pieces, to be reconquered in the following century by the more vigorous dynasty of Ramses. Meanwhile Ahknaton died, at the age of twenty-nine, and was eventually succeeded by his son-in-law, Tutankhaton, who reverted to the old form of worship and dropped the suffix Aton to become Tutankhamen.[1] He abandoned Tell el Amarna, which soon became a deserted city, and removed his court, amid popular enthusiasm, back to Thebes. The priesthood of Amon reigned supreme once more, and his name was restored to the walls of its temples, while that of Akhnaton was expunged from the records. Thus ended, after thirteen years, the romantic attempt to create an ancient Egyptian Utopia.

Tutankhamen was a frail youth, with refined features and long eyelashes, who died, after a brief reign, at the age of nineteen. No burial arrangements had been made for him, and he was interred, his funerary furniture piled in after him higgledy-piggledy, in a makeshift tomb of modest dimensions. It was overlooked by the professional tomb-robbers, who had left for the archaeologists of the future relatively little but the mummies of a few dozen Pharaohs and members of their families, and was discovered intact only in 1922 with all that it had originally contained. Its treasures, transferred to the Egyptian Museum in Cairo, revealed to a dazzled world a high degree of sophistication in the Pharaonic art of the fourteenth century B.C.

A circuit of the Cairo Museum is a consecutive procession through the three thousand years of ancient Egyptian history. Proceeding clockwise, we enter first the Old Kingdom, with its works of art from the pyramid cities of Sakkara, Giza and elsewhere. Its society, from the lower strata upwards, is freely represented in sculpture. First we see the servant class, naked figures, kneeling and squatting at their menial tasks — girls cooking cakes or kneading dough, a man straining beer through a sieve, another roasting a goose on a brazier — statuettes freely moulded and alive with movement. Occasionally there is a glimpse of them in relief, from a tomb, as of a spirited fight between two boatmen, one of whom is urging a looker-on to "crack him on his box!" while another cries, "Split open his back!"

---

[1] Sometimes transliterated as Tutankhamon or Tutankhamun.

A stratum above them are the "civil servants" and the nobility — a scribe sitting cross-legged, writing on a papyrus roll across his knees; a dwarf who was both a priest and an overseer of the wardrobe; a High Priest, who was also a general and a prince, seated beside his wife, who was a member of the Pharaonic family; a handsome chief baker with an athletic figure; the sturdy "sheikh" of a village — as the modern fellaheen identify him — carved out of wood, with a long staff in his hand. Thickset and muscular, roundheaded, bull-necked, broad-chested, and a trifle hunched, these early Egyptians give the impression of a strong, down-to-earth peasant race.

Their Pharaohs are a glorified version of them, royal but still human images. Cast with streamlined figures, idealised features, and stylized beards, they sit enthroned or stand erect, godlike in a hieratic pose in their aprons and headdresses, here between two goddesses, there sheltered by the wings of the falcon-headed Horus.

As our circuit proceeds through the Middle Kingdom, this regal and impersonal note starts to dominate. Gods and kings, whether in human or in animal form, prevail in the statuary over ordinary mortals. Figures grow more standardized in form, more conventional in posture, more severe in expression. The sculptor's technique becomes at once more finished and more academic. Hieroglyphics and mythical beasts crowd the sarcophagi and the stelae — the inscribed "tombstones." They contrast strongly with those of the Old Kingdom, which have rather an architectural character, as though reproducing in miniature the façades of the houses in which the dead once lived.

True art breaks through in the less formal portraits of officials and others, particularly in those carved out of wood; craftsmanship in the more stylized carving of animal and plant life. But in general the principle of authority overrides that of humanity. Through the New Kingdom this asserts itself until the period of Akhnaton, with its reversion to naturalism, and by reaction more aggressively afterwards. Meanwhile, however, the brief interim period of Tutankhamen reconciles academic convention with some of that freedom of invention which Amarna inspired.

Pursuing our chronological circuit, we find the treasures from Tutankhamen's tomb on the upper floor of the museum. What we have seen hitherto has reflected for us little of the interior and domestic environment of the ancient Egyptians. Almost nothing — thanks to centuries of contemporary and subsequent looting of tombs — has survived to prepare us for the developments in the applied and decorative arts, running parallel with those of sculpture and painting, which now bursts upon us in the furnishing of Tutankhamen's tomb. Here is a richness comparable in kind (but hardly in style) to that of the palaces of some prince of the Renaissance or of the ages of Louis XV in France or George IV in England. Here spread before us is virtually everything — furniture, statuary, ornaments, and household utensils, glass and faience, vases and jars of alabaster, *objets d'art* (often of sacred significance), toilet articles, sporting weapons, and other implements — such as the palace of a Pharaoh of this second Golden Age of Egypt must have contained.

Luxurious, often over elaborate, not always in impeccable taste, these are nonetheless the products of a supreme craftsmanship, allied to inventiveness and skill in the use of materials, a sense of elegance and a consummate virtuosity in decoration and design — a combination of the talents of artist and craftsman which here and there achieves true art.

Notable among these is the wooden throne of the King, which resembles an upright chair coated with gold leaf and with a multicoloured inlay of silver, faience, glass, and stone. Its legs and feet are the legs and claws of lions, surmounted in front with their heads. Its arms take the form of crowned, winged serpents. Its backpanel is embossed with a painting, richly coloured in blue and silver and umber against gold, of the King and the Queen with the rays of the Amarna sun still shining down upon them. The back of another chair, made of cedarwood, is carved with an openwork relief of the King, seated like an idol among his gods and solar symbols. Designed like an elaborate campstool, with a seat of imitation leopard skin and ducks' heads for legs, the back of a third is intricately inlaid with a marquetry of ebony, ivory, and other precious materials.

On the lid of an inlaid ivory chest the young King is portrayed with his Queen amid a luxuriant profusion of lotus and papyrus flowers, while two maidservants kneel to gather for them the mandrake and other plants. The panels of another chest, which contained his linen, are painted with scenes as in oriental miniatures, but swifter in movement, in which the King in his chariot hunts gazelle, deer, and ostriches, and slays his enemies in battle. Carved on one of his numerous gilded shields is a lively portrait of him, slaying a couple of lions which he holds by the tail.

Gold leaf shines sumptuous and clear from the furniture of Tutankhamen's tomb, liberally applied in particular to those pieces which have a sacred significance. For gold was the divine metal, the

Edfu. Ptolemaic statue of Horus, falcon-god of the Sky, in the courtyard
of his Temple.

Roger Wood

Nile felucca.

Henry G. Fischer

Dimitr

Delta Village.

Roger Wood

Sinai, St.
Catherine's
Monastery.
Mosaic of
Christ in the
Church of the
Transfiguration.

Henry G. Fischer

Abydos, centre of pilgrimage for the devotees of the god Osiris. Relief in
the Temple of Ramses II.

Sinai. Icon of the 'Ladder of Climax', ascending to Heaven, in the Library of St. Catherine's Monastery.

incorruptible "flesh of the sun" and of his galaxy of gods and god-desses, and was not the Pharaoh himself a god, "a golden mountain lighting the whole country like the god of the horizon"? A plentiful use of gold should ensure Tutankhamen's divine survival.

Thus the mask which covered his mummified head is of gold, moulded to his likeness, with lapis lazuli eyebrows and eyelids, and a headdress of gold inlaid with bands of blue glass. The coffin which contained his mummy is of thick gold, moulded in the guise of Osiris to the shape of his figure. It was itself contained in two more coffins, wooden but coated with gold, of which the largest remains in the tomb, with the mummy inside it. All three rested in the sarcophagus, on a gilded bier as elegant as a Regency couch. Gold coated are the four shrines as big as furniture vans, decorated with scenes of the underworld, which, one within the other, contained the sarcophagus. A statue of the King, from the tomb, has eyelids and eyebrows of gold.

The divine metal gleams everywhere — in a small gilded shrine on a silver sledge, its panels decorated with a portrait of the King on a shooting trip; in the decoration of chariots and harness; in sun-boats designed for the Underworld; in sandals, daggers, and breastplates; in rings, scarabs, bracelets and necklaces. Precious stones, too, abound in the jewellery: lapis lazuli, amethyst, carnelian, turquoise, chalce-dony, feldspar.

Finished workmanship and an ingenious eye for decorative mo-tifs distinguish each object — boomerangs, throwing-sticks, horns, knives, scimitars, staffs and walking-sticks, headrests, handmirrors, scent bottles, pen cases, gaming boards, knuckle bones, together with such practical utensils as a papyrus burnisher and a fire-lighter, operated by friction. A bow is encrusted with filigree gold; another has a case tipped with blue faience and decorated in gold leaf and bark, while the points of its arrows are of ivory.

A child's armchair is of ebony and ivory, with gold-coated arms. Rattles are of gilded bronze, with metal rods in the form of serpents. Amulets are exquisite bibelots, figurines of gods and goddesses are elegant drawing-room ornaments. An ivory scent-box, in the form of a goose with movable wings, might have been conceived by Fabergé. A fan is of ostrich feathers with an ivory handle, carved with the names of the King. Decorative touches of wit are groups of bound and prostrate prisoners, carved on a footstool and painted on the seat of a chair.

The civilization which these objects illuminate endured for two or three hundred years more, declining gradually towards the end of the Ramessid dynasty and more rapidly afterwards. The priesthood grew more and more powerful until, in the eleventh century, they established a Pharaoh of their own on the throne. Gradually the North and the South fell apart into a series of independent but ephemeral principalities at odds with each other. As the country thus weakened it fell beneath the sway of the foreigner — the Libyans, the Ethiopians, the Assyrians, and the Persians, from whom it was finally liberated in 332 B.C. by Alexander the Great. He founded Alexandria, which now became the capital of Egypt, remaining however a Greek city, remote in spirit from the rest of the country.

Arts and crafts meanwhile had declined, but under Alexander's successors, the Ptolemies, they revived in a last brief Renaissance. The Greeks adopted and adapted for themselves some of the Egyptian gods, and new temples were built at Philae, Edfu, Komombo, and elsewhere. Ptolemaic architecture, conservative in its adherence to the Egyptian idiom, imitated that of the Egyptian past, but imitated it well, so that Edfu in particular, still intact as it is, gives a gratifying impression of what an earlier Pharaonic temple was like. The reliefs in these temples have a coarseness alien to the old canons of sculpture, and in their feminine figures a rounded sensuality, breaking free of the discretion and restraint of the past, which nonetheless gives them life.

Through the consecutive marriages of Julius Ceasar and Mark Antony to Cleopatra — a pure Macedonian Greek of untold wealth, since all Egypt was her personal possession — Egypt finally came under Roman rule, with Octavian crowned as Pharaoh. Each subsequent Roman Emperor, though he left the country in the hands of a provincial Viceroy, automatically assumed the divine rank. The gradual decline of Rome coincided with a decline in the traditional Egyptian beliefs. Hellenism failed to make an impact upon Egypt, and soon a Christian era dawned.

REFERENCES

E. Wallis Budge.   *A Short History of the Egyptian People.* 1914.
Adolf Erman.   *A Handbook of Egyptian Religion.* 1907.
Georges Posener.   *A Dictionary of Egyptian Civilization.* 1962.
Arthur Weigall.   *A Short History of Ancient Egypt.* 1935.
Jon Manchip White.   *Everyday Life in Ancient Egypt.* 1963.

PART 2 CHRISTIAN EGYPT

Chapter 6
The Copts

The Nile Delta fans outwards above Memphis, the old capital, and Cairo, the new, towards Alexandria, the capital of the Greeks and the Romans and eventually the Christians, on the Mediterranean Sea. It is named for its shape, from the Greek letter Delta. Washed not only by the sea but by the sands of the desert, it was seen by the classical world as an "island" between the two continents of Asia and Africa.

The Delta is a countryside hard to traverse, crisscrossed and scored by a confusion of ditches and irrigation canals. They intercept and distribute the Nile waters, saturating the soil to make a triangle of deep green fertility, and so tapping the great river that it ebbs away into the sea at Rosetta and Damietta in two streams now of no very formidable volume. Its precious mud, nonetheless, clouds the Mediterranean for many miles offshore, making a dull stain, visible today from an aircraft and, in the time of Herodotus, causing mariners to bring up mud with a sounding-line while still a day's sail from land.

The countless villages of the Delta, each a huddle of mud houses beneath a cluster of palms, stand out like islands themselves in this fruit-ful "sea." Dovecots, tall as lighthouses, punctuate the landscape, store-houses of organic manure to reinforce the life-giving ooze from the Nile. The broad flat willow-shaded landscape teems with life, horned buffaloes wallowing balefully in the muddy waters while the fellaheen, the ancient peasant population of Egypt, crouch over the fields in their hundreds of thousands, working to sow and to reap and to harvest the fruits of the alluvial soil.

The Delta is barred, before it reaches the Mediterranean, by a chain of broad saline lakes, running parallel to the sea and divided from it only by the road to Rosetta — a road fringed by sand-flats and by a long ridge of dunes, liberally sprinkled with mimosa and thorn. Here is a different natural element, a luminous land of reeds, where aquatic birds abound and where fishermen cast their nets in the shallow waters from pointed boats, like gondolas. Between the sea and the most westerly lake, called Mareotis by the Greeks and Mariut today, there juts out a long narrow peninsula, its limestone reefs forming two natural harbours. Along this is built the city of Alexandria.

Its conception was, in Gibbon's words, a "noble design" of Alexander the Great. He himself chose the site and planned the city, as an emporium for trade and a Greek cultural outpost, accessible by sea to his native land of Macedonia. But he never lived to see it built. Alexandria was to grow up without him, while his body lay buried — as it may lie buried still — beneath its central crossroads. It grew into a fine Greco-Roman cosmopolis, a classical maritime capital, governing Egypt but so separated from it, in spirit by its Hellenic culture, in geography by the waters of its lake, then a navigable sea, that its inhabitants would speak of travelling "from Alexandria to Egypt."

Its street-plan, dictated as it still is by a site which has length but not breadth, was traced on the ground for Alexander's preliminary inspection with flour, since the architects ran out of chalk. Before it the Pharos, part lighthouse, part fortress, towered up to a height of nearly five hundred feet from a rock between the two harbours. A four-storied wonder, technological and aesthetic, of the classical world, it was likened by Herodotus to "a mountain planted in the sea, surrounded by another sun."

Alexandria was a gleaming white city, as it is today, but enriched by a wealth of fine classical architecture, none of which has survived. Two "cities within a city" contained respectively the buildings of the royal palace, with its government offices, and those of the *mouseion* or museum. This grew into a great centre of learning in science and literature, far outstripping its prototype in Athens, and embodying a renowned library of half a million volumes.

On a hill in the centre, dedicated before the time of Alexander to the worship of Osiris, the Greeks built the Serapeum, a temple dedicated to Serapis, who was a Hellenic compound of Osiris and Apis. When the first library was burnt in a rising against the Romans, a second was installed in its precincts. Only a warren of underground galleries and chambers survives from the shrine, crowned with a tall Roman column of granite, called Pompey's Pillar but in fact inscribed to the Emperor Diocletian.

The rest of the Serapeum, including the second library, was destroyed in its turn by the devotees of a new cult, that of the Christians. The destruction was in a sense a symbolic revenge for the traditional martyrdom, by the devotees of Serapis, of St. Mark the Evangelist. He is supposed to have introduced Christianity into Egypt, first converting a Jewish shoemaker, then founding a Christian oratory on the seashore. Denouncing one of the pagan festivals as "idolatrous," St. Mark was dragged through the streets of the city for two days in succession with a rope round his neck, and finally thrown into prison, where, fortified by the vision of an angel, he expired.

Earlier the Virgin and Child, with Joseph, had fled into Egypt, settling for a while at the Egyptian township of Babylon, on the Nile opposite Memphis. Here legends record miracles of healing, which the sacred infant unconsciously performed. A spring of pure water still exists at Mataria, in which His clothes are said to have been washed on the journey by Mary; in Heliopolis nearby the apocryphal gospels record that His entry into the temple caused the idols to fall to the ground.

The Christian cult, nonetheless, developed slowly. For some time it made little stir in the Greek world, where it was generally seen simply as an offshoot of Judaism. Outside Alexandria the natives of Egypt, "a people distinguished," to Gibbon, "by a sullen inflexibility of temper," at first "entertained the new doctrine with coldness and reluctance; and . . . it was rare to meet an Egyptian who had surmounted his early prejudices in favour of the sacred animals of his country." But by the end of the second century the Christians had grown, in the city itself, into an industrious and prosperous community, attracting the unfavourable notice of the Roman authorities by its refusal to worship the Emperor as a god.

Thus the persecution of Christians began. At first — despite their claims to the contrary — it was on a modest enough scale. Under the Emperor Decius a mere ten men and seven women were martyred for the profession of Christian beliefs. But the Emperor Diocletian resolved to stamp out the seditious cult altogether and initiated an Era of Martyrs — which had precisely the opposite effect. The reduction of his Christian subjects to slavery, the degradation and imprisonment of their clergy, the suppression and demolition of their churches and the burning of their sacred books was to ensure, by reaction, the survival of the faith, until it became, under Constantine, the official religion of the Empire.

The Egyptians thus passed from the domination of pagan Rome to that of Christian Byzantium. "The zeal of those barbarians," as Gibbon described them, "obeyed the prevailing impulsion; the cities of Egypt were filled with bishops, and the deserts of Thebais swarmed with hermits." With the turn of the tide it became the lot of the pagans to endure persecution, a process which culminated early in the fifth century in the lynching, by a horde of fanatical monks, of the learned Hypatia, a Greek female professor at the University of the Mouseion, who thus won legendary fame as a martyr to the Greek ideal.

Such was the apotheosis of Christian monasticism as founded in the deserts of Egypt. It had grown initially from a cult of asceticism prevalent among pagan Egyptian and Jewish communities which pursued the Platonic ideal of self-denial and purity. It had increased under the persecutions, when refugees sought to escape, together with less pious fugitives from the taxgatherer and the police, into the desert, there dwelling as hermits and anchorites in caves and disused tombs.

The first of these to attract attention was St. Paul the Hermit, who is said by tradition to have led the solitary life in a cave between the Nile and the Red Sea, but who may never in fact have existed. An authentic historical figure was St. Antony, who may thus be regarded as the founder of Christian monasticism. Antony, an illiterate son of a prosperous family in a Theban village, sold all he had on the death of his parents and gave to the poor. Soon afterwards he withdrew into the Eastern Desert, where he lived for twenty years, successively in a tomb, in a disused fort, and in a cave in the mountains above the Red Sea.

Here he wrestled alone in his conscience with the diabolical spirits which were known to inhabit these regions. He persistently crushed out the desires of the flesh, fasting for days at a time, denying himself sleep and resting only on the bare ground, scorning all rules of hygiene, earning fame as worker of miracles, and eventually dying at the age of a hundred and five. The force of his example was such that other ascetics gathered in large numbers around him, competing with one another for "records" in austerity. They so multiplied after his death that the deserts of Egypt became virtually an immense colony of monks, filling whole towns and forming monastic communities which took to housing themselves in the temples of the ancient Egyptians.

Most of these thousands of monks were poor and ignorant, with rough ways and scant intellect. But those who lived up to the Christian vocation "sang Psalms, loved reading, fasted, prayed, rejoiced in the hope of things to come, laboured in almsgiving, and preserved love and harmony one with another . . . there was neither the evil-doer, nor the injured, nor the reproaches of the taxgatherer; but a multitude of ascetics; and the one purpose of them all was to aim at virtue." So wrote St. Athanasius, for long Bishop of Alexandria, who was responsible for introducing the monastic life to Rome. Here, as Gibbon describes it, "the strange and savage appearance of these Egyptians excited, at first, horror and contempt, and at length applause and zealous imitation," until palaces, villas, temples, and even parts of the Forum itself were transformed into monasteries.

The initial upsurge of monasticism was essentially an Egyptian, not a Greek, phenomenon. Antony and the majority of his followers spoke only the Egyptian language and were anti-Greek in their sentiments. The Church that had been nurtured and united by persecution thus became, with recognition, fiercely divided in schism and discord, so that the Christian Greek Empire of Byzantium grew to be as much resented by the native Egyptians as that of pagan Rome had been.

Theologically, the conflict was between differing conceptions of the nature of Christ, as Son of God. How far was he human, how far divine? The Greeks on the one hand, with their background of classical philosophy, sought through their protagonist, Arius, to stress the human nature of Christ, thus bringing him nearer to man; the Egyptians, more abstract, more oriental in their habits of thought, accepted only his divine nature. Their mouthpiece was Athanasius, to whom the Arians were pagans, worshipping the Creature, whereas his own followers worshipped only the Creator. These doctrinal battles were fought out in two successive councils of the Church, inconclusively at Nicaea in the fourth century A.D., and more conclusively at Chalcedon in the fifth. Here it was decreed that Christ had two natures. It was a decree which the Egyptians, uncompromising in their insistence on the single nature, refused to accept. They adhered instead to the heresy which became known as Monophysitism.

The effect of this adherence was largely political. From now onwards the Egyptians were in overt rebellion against the Byzantine Emperor, rejecting his spiritual, and only grudgingly accepting

his temporal, authority. It was as much a racial as a religious rebellion, a species of nationalist movement with the Church at its head. The
Greeks of Alexandria were persecuted as an alien minority, and
dwindled accordingly. The Egyptians came to see themselves as
Copts — the name "Egyptian" rendered as *Aiguptios* by the Greeks,
and later abbreviated to Kibt, otherwise Copt. The Coptic Church,
regarded by Byzantium as heretical, continued to regard itself as the
true repository of orthodox Christianity, and remains to this day out
of communion with the rest of Christendom. The Copts themselves
remain a religious and to some extent a racial minority in Egypt.
They still claim, with some justification, to be the only true descendants of the ancient Egyptians.

Today the religious traditions and artistic works of the Copts survive
at their best within the fortress of Babylon, in a district now known
as Old Cairo. Standing on the southern outskirts of the present-day
capital and across the Nile from the Pharaonic capital of Memphis,
the fortress embodies, in its towers and walls, the few remaining
architectural remains of that Roman occupation which its founders
so heartily detested. Built by the Emperor Trajan, on the site of a
former Pharaonic colony of Babylonian captives, it was strategically
situated, commanding the southern apex of the Delta and, by a bridge
of boats across the river, the desert road to Alexandria from Palestine
and Arabia.

   This was the route by which an invader might come and by which
Christianity came, in the persons first of the Holy Family, then of St.
Mark, with St. Peter. Probably it was here, amid the Jewish colony
of Babylon, that St. Peter wrote his first epistle and St. Mark his
gospel. Babylon's Jews were converted to Christianity at an early
date; their synagogue, in which Joseph and Mary may have worshipped, was turned into a church, and in due time Babylon came to
replace Alexandria as the main centre of the Coptic religion.

   It was here, within the fortress walls of their former persecutors,
the Romans, that the Christians were to take refuge from a later
persecution, that of the Moslem invaders. Here they built churches,
in which they continued to worship when the Arabs had destroyed
those outside. Here, using an otherwise dead language which is
virtually that of the ancient Egyptians, and a ritual deriving from the
earliest Christian times, they worship still.

   The walls containing their churches, Roman below and Byzantine
above, are broken by two circular bastions and by a water-gate. This

gives no longer onto a channel of the Nile, as before, since the channel has changed its course with time, but still onto its original quay,
where the water seeps in with a high flood. At a variety of levels,
perched on the ramparts or buried within, they are Christian basilicas,
some of them fourth-century foundations — long barrel-vaults dark
through the passage of centuries, aisles and sanctuaries shadowy in
the dim diffused light, their classical columns painted and begrimed
but revealing traces, now of a Cross, now of a Coptic inscription,
now of the figure of a saint.

These churches rank among the oldest in existence still in use as
such. Simple in ornament and unchanging in atmosphere, they seem
pervaded still by the spirit of the Holy Family, the Apostles, the
early Christian martyrs. One, older perhaps than the rest, built twenty
feet below the present level of the ground and hence at the level of
the Roman foundations, occupies the traditional site of the house in
which the Holy Family lodged, and which must have become a place
of worship soon after their time. Today it is the crypt of the larger
and later church, above, of the fourth-century martyrs, St. Sergius and
St. Bacchus. Its infrequent services commemorate the Nativity and
the Flight into Egypt. Its baptismal ceremonies are blessed by asso-
ciations with the Christ child, and by the thought that the waters of
its font may flow from the original source where the Holy Family
drew its own water.

Associated with the Apostle St. Mark is a ruined church, now
inaccessible, built like several others for security, within the thickness of the fortress walls. Other churches in Babylon commemorate,
in the icons and carvings of their inlaid screens, the warrior saints of
the Copts of the Era of Martyrs. Here is the Egyptian St. George,
whose dragon was Diocletian, and who, with the aid of prayer,
resisted throughout an entire night the seductions of an imperial
concubine and had converted her to Christianity by morning. Here
are St. Dimiana, a martyr to Diocletian, who had her tortured and
beheaded with a whole convent of fellow-nuns, for refusing him
submission by sacrifice; St. Mercurius, a victim of the persecutions of
Decius, clad in shining armour with two swords crossed above his
head, who may well be the Greek god Mercury in a Christian guise;
above all the Archangel Michael, who, with the blessing of a fourth-
century Pope, inherited the devotions formerly due to a classical idol
and now ranks as the guardian of the Delta itself.

The Copts, simple and untutored natives of Egypt, isolated from
the world in their monasteries, had no outstanding talent for art.

Their painting was primitive, their carving crude. The Coptic Museum, within these walls, reveals an art which embodies successively Greco-Roman, Byzantine, and Syrian Christian motifs. Much of it was imported from Greece itself. Only gradually do the Christian symbols start to appear. The Cross imposes itself severely on a familiar profusion of classical foliage; saints supplant gods and angels goddesses, human figures carved in artless contrast to a stylized framework of natural motifs.

The stonecarving of the Copts has a certain ingenuous charm. Their woodcarving, on the other hand, in church screens, doors, and lecterns fashioned from a variety of woods and inlaid with ivory, ebony, or mother-of-pearl, shows often an intricate refinement of craftsmanship. Doubtless influenced by the Arabs, it comes more to life through its incorporation of human and animal forms into the strictly geometrical Moslem designs.

These Coptic craftsmen show skill in the carving of ivories. But where they shine at their brightest is in the embroidery of textiles, the fine linens and wools which the ancient Egyptians had been weaving for centuries past. The tunics they made from them in the fourth century replaced the togas of the Romans. They were used often as funeral shrouds, and have since been disinterred from a variety of Coptic graveyards. The Copts adorned them freely with designs in bright colours, harmonizing Christian with classical motifs — solemn saints, lively dancers, as though from a Greek vase — in decorative patterns uniquely their own.

Much of this art had its origins in the early monastic communities. And a number of these still thrive in the deserts of Egypt, their way of life as of worship little changed for a thousand years and more.

Chapter 7

The Monastic Communities

The road from Cairo to Alexandria runs, as it may have done since the days of the Romans, along the fringe of the Delta, crossing a landscape clean-cut in its contrast between desert and sown. Halfway between the two cities, some miles to the desert side of it, lies the depression of the Wadi Natrun. Once possibly an outlet of the Nile, it is now a valley with a chain of shallow lakes, gleaming saline in the sand. Here salt and soda — as used in the process of mummification — have been worked since the days of the ancient Egyptians. Around the lakes a modern Egyptian government labours to make the desert bloom, sinking wells and planting appropriate crops. Beyond, their high walls breasting the wastes of the desert as those of ships breast the waves of the sea, there survives a group of the world's oldest Christian monasteries.

Built like fortresses, they seem at first sight to be abandoned and empty. No sound comes from within their Defensive walls to break the silence of the desert around them. Then the visitor tugs at a bell. A cautious pale face with a fringe of beard appears at a slit of a window above the gateway. After a scrutiny it disappears. In a few moments a monk opens a door, on creaking hinges, and a bell clangs out from above to greet the stranger.

What he finds within is a sequence of haphazard courtyards, their buildings rising as it were organically from the stones of the desert without. Here monks and their masons have built as though by the light of nature, from the local materials, and with little change in style since hermits first gathered for security within such walled communities. Their huddling domes and wandering walls and clambering outside stairways make patterns so fluid that no line seems wholly straight and no curve wholly true. But the asymmetry conceals a traditional order, at once sacred and functional.

Four monasteries only survive, with a few score of monks, from among the fifty or more that once furnished the desert with a population of some five thousand Christian souls. Each of them — those of Abu Makar (St. Macarius), Anba Bishoi (his disciple), Baramus (the Roman Brothers), and Suriani (the Syrians) — contains churches and chapels built and enlarged in successive centuries between the fourth and the fourteenth, composite places of worship which are often more spacious than those confined within the narrower limits of Babylon.

The Great Church of St. Macarius is in fact four churches in one, a spreading irregular perspective of high rough walls and pointed arches and rounded domes. All provide a cool refuge from the burning heat of the desert, their walls, as protection against sandstorms, pierced only with occasional slits of windows, covered with coloured glass or with a tracery of stucco to admit filtering beams of light. In the sanctuaries and chapels there survive traces of early murals, portraying the fathers of Coptic monasticism or scenes from the life of Christ. As time goes on they begin to reveal, like the woodwork screens, a new influence — that of the Islamic conqueror.

Sparse gardens, watered from wells beneath the surface of the desert, provide the monks with a few vegetables grown in the shade of tattered palmtrees and tamarinds — of which one vast and aged specimen, in the garden of Suriani, is declared to have sprung from the staff of an especially holy anchorite, taking root where he left it outside an abbot's cell. The cells of the monks, with low doorways and roofs hardly higher than those of caves, open onto the gardens and courtyards. So do their kitchens, roofed with a progression of small domes. Their long low vaulted refectories have built-in benches and tables of stone or brick — one of them scattered still with loaves as hard as stones, which no monk has cared to remove.

But the most individual feature of each monastery is the keep, towering above the walls with hardly a window to light it, with a door at mid-level and only a drawbridge — formerly only a rope or a ladder — as link with the surrounding rooftops. When the barbarians of the desert — the Bedouin of today — raided and plundered the monasteries, the monks withdrew into these fortified towers, which were built around wells and equipped to stand a siege. In their basements are storerooms, flour mills, oil presses; on the other floors living quarters, refectories, and chapels, unkempt chambers perhaps decorated with murals which are barely to be seen through the gloom.

The most civilized of these monasteries was that of the Syrians, Suriani. It differs from those of the Copts in the greater refinement of its frescoes and the carving of its stucco and woodwork, but above all in the library which gave it a wide reputation as a centre of learning. These Syrian monks were supported by a group of merchants from Mesopotamia, who had settled in Old Cairo, and furnished them with manuscripts inscribed in the Syriac language. But their main benefactor was their own tenth-century abbot, named Moses, who returned laden with Syriac manuscripts from a three-year journey in Syria and Mesopotamia. Other benefactors enriched the monastery with similar gifts, until its library's manuscripts were numbered in thousands. They included the oldest dated book in the world, a fifth-century manuscript from Edessa, an early centre of Christianity; and fragments of a Bible written in the fifth century at Diyarbekir, on the Tigris.

The library of Suriani, here in the wastes of the Egyptian desert, thus became one of the richest in the Eastern Christian world, and indeed, as it happened, the main repository of the fruits of the knowledge of the Mesopotamian monks. It was a knowledge which embraced the works of ancient Greece, of the great classical thinkers on philosophy and science, which these monks had zealously translated first into Syriac, then into Arabic and Latin, thus serving as intermediaries to preserve them for posterity in the Western world. Gradually, from the seventeenth century onwards, European scholars became aware of this treasure trove. Some manuscripts found their way to libraries in Milan and Paris. In the eighteenth century the Pope came into the market and a further collection reached the Vatican Library, though a large part of it was lost, together with the papal emmissary, when the boat carrying them sank in the Nile.

It was finally the British Museum which secured the lion's share of the surviving books and manuscripts. This followed a visit to Suriani by Robert Curzon in 1833. He was allowed to take away a number of ancient Coptic manuscript sheets which he found lying on the floor or serving as covers for preserve jars. Finally, by plying a convivial abbot with generous potions of a strong sweet cordial, he was able to buy from him several Syriac books which he had unearthed from the depths of the oil cellar. This stimulated the museum trustees to secure a Treasury grant and thus to buy from the monastery most of its remaining manuscripts. They form today the bulk of its Syriac collection.

Dependent on Suriani for a time was the Monastery of St. Antony, the "father foundation" of monasticism, in the Red Sea mountains. It was built close to the lonely spot where the saint had his last hermitage, but some two centuries after his death, and by Greek, not Coptic monks, who regarded it askance. St. Antony's, built amid palms beneath an ochre-coloured mountain, is the largest of all the Egyptian monasteries. In effect it is a small fortified town, now sparsely inhabited, with a mile-long circuit of thirty-foot walls and a parapet walk around the top, punctuated with watertowers and turrets where the monks mounted guard. The Copts took it over in the Middle Ages, when it was famed for its library and its staff of expert copyists. But eventually the Moslems sacked and destroyed it, after slaughtering all its monks. Beyond its mountain is the smaller and more intimate monastery of St. Antony's predecessor, the hermit St. Paul.

Of all the monasteries of Egypt, the most renowned is St. Catherine's, a Greek, not a Coptic, foundation, buried deep in the heart of the mountains and deserts of the Sinai Peninsula, which separates the Nile Valley from Palestine. This was the wilderness of the forty-year wanderings of the children of Israel, following the Exodus from the Delta which seems to have occurred during the reign of Tutankhamen. Hence the region of the Sinai monastery has links with the Judaism of the Old Testament as with the Christianity of the New. According to tradition, it was here beyond the Red Sea, amid the rugged southern rocks of the peninsula, that Moses first dwelt and later brought his host, hearing the word of God from the burning bush and receiving the tablets of the Law from Mount Sinai.

This tradition may well be false. A close study of the Bible in connection with the geography of the country drew Major C. S. Jarvis, a modern governor of Sinai, to the conclusion that the Israelites travelled not by the southern route, across the Red Sea from Suez, but by a northern route inland, following the line of the Mediterranean coast. Here they would have found a more fertile area for settlement, providing not merely manna — a form of deposit left by insects on the branches of the tamarisk bush — but the grain and oil crops and the grazing for oxen and sheep and goats which they needed and certainly found. Moreover it is to this region in the north, not to the south, that the migrating quails, which helped to nourish the Israelites, have always come, clouds of them making landfall from the Mediterranean Sea in a state of exhaustion, which makes them easy to capture.

Again this is a region visited in heavy weather by "pillars of cloud" from the east, which at night seem to become "pillars of fire" through the reflections upon them from the torches of caravans. Finally the "Red Sea" of the Exodus, which engulfed the Egyptian army, is more likely — and in translation from the Hebrew more literally — the "Sea of Reeds." This could well be Lake Bardawil, just inland from the Mediterranean coast, normally dry, as when the Israelites crossed it, but liable suddenly to be flooded by a cloudburst, which could easily have bogged down Pharaoh's chariots and drowned many of his men in pursuit of the Israelite horde. Tradition, however, persists in associating the Exodus with the more barren and precipitous country around the apex of the peninsula. And indeed its mountains are grandiose and inspiring enough to serve as an appropriate setting for Genesis.

The traveller of today crosses into Sinai no longer by the Red Sea but by a ferry across the Suez Canal some miles north of Suez — usually, in view of the length of the journey, before dawn, when the canal is lit like an arterial road with the traffic lights of the ships passing down it in convoy. Thence his route runs southeastwards across a desert slowly reddening to the east with the light of the rising sun, to strike the Red Sea once more at Abu Zenima. This is a mining port, called after a Moslem saint, from which the ancient Egyptians exported turquoises, malachite, and a wealth of precious metals mined in the jagged red rocks, as manganese is mined and exported today.

From here the road turns inland, gradually climbing up the Wadi Feiran, from a landscape of sand and limestone eroded into soft architectural shapes to a harsher landscape of gravel and granite. Two of its more spectacular outcrops are identified respectively with the rock which Moses struck to bring forth water (no uncommon phenomenon in this country of hidden springs) and that other rock (now covered with Hebrew inscriptions) which barred his way and was thus cleft in twain "as though it had been but a piece of flesh." Halfway to the monastery is the well-watered oasis of Feiran, luxuriant with palm-trees and olives and vines. In Old Testament times it was a city of the Amalekites, in Roman times an episcopal see, with a cathedral and a population of anchorites, housed in caves and cells which still honeycomb the alluvial rocks of Mount Serbal.

Above the oasis the landscape closes in on the road. Mountains, treeless and birdless but for an occasional circling buzzard, rear up on either side of it, bare and malignant but bright with the scintillant strata of feldspar and porphyry, viridian and chrome. As the sunlight wanes an air of fantasy suffuses the landscape, the rocks rearing higher into shapes more ethereal, their vivid reds and greens and yellows softened and transmuted into a roseate pink.

Loneliness haunts this giant-made world until suddenly, unexpectedly, at the head of a long red-shadowed valley, life once more confronts the traveller — the man-made granite walls of a monastic fortress, wedged at the foot of two towering slopes; a man-planted garden of cypress and olive beside it; finally, man himself, Greek man, bearded and cassocked, waving a hand from the battlements, then descending to open a massive door to the stranger.

Anchorites fled into this forbidding, hallowed land from the fourth century onwards, settling wherever they could find springs of water, in scattered hermitages of which many are still marked by the ruins of chapels. They led a hunted life, exchanging the persecution of the Romans for that of the Saracens, the Bedouin hordes of the region, who once butchered a community of forty in a place still named to commemorate the massacre. For their protection, as devotees not of the Coptic but of the Greek Orthodox faith, the Emperor Justinian built them this monastery, into which they moved from the surrounding mountains. This served the double purpose of providing the monks with a secure refuge and the Emperor himself with a useful link in his imperial communications.

Thoughfully, the Emperor furnished the monks with an army of vassals, from Egypt and the Black Sea mountains, to guard them and serve their needs. Their descendants, Moslems now but some still with a trace of Greece or Rome in their features, perform the role to this day, as paid servants, supervised by four sheikhs whom the monks appoint, and derided by the local Bedouin as the monastery "slaves."

The monastery was built in the sixth century, around a Chapel of the Burning Bush founded two hundred years earlier by St. Helena, the mother of Constantine. On the holy spot a bush still grows, a species of fruitless bramble, propagated by cuttings from what is said to be the original root; and a later chapel still stands, in which a light burns perpetually, while the tablets of the Law are still embedded in its walls — or so the monks declare.

Sinai. St. Catherine's Monastery, at the foot of Mount Moses.

Cairo. Courtyard and minaret of the Mosque of Ibn Tulun.

Cairo. Courtyard of the Mosque of al Azhar.

A. F. Kersting

A. F. Kersting

Above: Cairo. The Citadel of Saladin and the Mosque of Sultan Hasan, at the foot of it.

Below: Cairo. The Mausoleum of Sultan Barkuk, in the 'City of the Dead.'

Originally, adhering to the Mosaic legend, the monastery was called that of the Transfiguration, or of the Colloquy, in which the Lord spoke to Moses. But in the eleventh century it became the monastery of St. Catherine, the Alexandrine saint who (if indeed she ever existed) was broken, in the reign of Diocletian, on the "catherine" wheel and transported by angels to be buried on a peak above the monastery which bears her name. Bones which may have been hers were later unearthed, and some of her relics found their way, famed as sovereign remedies for pain, to the Western Christian world. The monastery suffered little from the Arab invasions, since Mohammed, once visiting it as a camel-boy, was believed to have granted it his protection. Hence, within the walls, the minaret of a mosque rises side by side with the belfry of the church.

Alone among the buildings, rebuilt through the centuries, this church has artistic and historical value. It is a basilica, never ruined and thus dating back, at its earliest, to the sixth century, the time of Justinian. Entered by two successive doors carved out of cypress-wood, the first Arab in workmanship but adorned by subsequent pilgrims with the arms of Crusaders, the second truly Byzantine in style and in feeling, the church is upheld by massive lotus-headed columns of granite, injudiciously painted. Darkness pervades the interior, for it is lit only by candles which shed a warm flickering light upon gilded icons and a profusion of ostrich eggs and other ornaments which hang from the ceiling.

Beyond the rich iconostasis, glowing gold in the half-dome of the apse, is the monastery's masterpiece, a sixth-century Byzantine mosaic of the Transfiguration, which gives the church its name. Blending Old and New Testament motifs, it depicts, in the hieratic style familiar in Santa Sophia in Istanbul, a white-robed Christ transfigured in a blinding light before, on the one hand, Moses and Elijah and, on the other, the Apostles Peter and James and John, framed by medallions of other Old Testament prophets. On either side of the arch are mosaic panels in which Moses removes his sandals before the burning bush and receives the tablets of stone in his hands.

Outstanding among the treasures of St. Catherine's are its icons, two thousand in number. Painted in the monastery or brought by pilgrims and others from every part of the Byzantine world, they cover the whole span of its icon painting, preserving continuity from the Golden Age of Justinian through the Dark Age of iconoclasm, with its destruction of images, to the artistic Renaissance which followed it, preceding the collapse of the Empire. For the early icons of Sinai, isolated as the monastery was by Islam in this remote Christian outpost, escaped destruction and survive as a unique and unbroken collection.

No Greek painting in existence excels, for example, the portrait here of St. Peter, with a bunch of keys in one hand and a staff in the other, his grave features revealing at once his reflective mind and his restless temper. Other paintings, recently cleaned and restored to show colouring as brilliant and luminous as that of enamel, bring to life, in the restrained classic style of Byzantium, such familiar religious scenes as the baptism of Christ in the Jordan, the raising of Lazarus from the dead, St. John the Evangelist weeping at the Crucifixion, and the ascent of an archbishop and his monks by a ladder to heaven, while winged black devils tug at them with pitchforks and catch those who fall.

But the pride of the monastery is its library, with its thousands of manuscripts in a dozen languages, many of them illuminated with fine Byzantine miniatures. Most of them date from the ninth and tenth centuries. These literary rarities include the oldest known translation of the Bible, probably of the second century, from Greek into Syriac, and the travelbook of a sixth-century tourist from Alexandria, illustrated with his own quaint drawings.

The most priceless of its treasures was the fourth-century Codex Sinaiticus, the oldest known Greek manuscript of the Bible, part of which was found in a wastepaper basket and rescued from burning by a German philologist, von Tischendorf, in 1844. Returning to the monastery fifteen years later, he discovered the rest of it and took the complete manuscript away to Russia, with a promise to return it. Instead it was presented to the Tsar and eventually sold by the Soviet Government to the British Museum for £100,000, half of which was contributed by public subscription.

Less than twenty aging monks remain in St. Catherine's Monastery today. They live on a sparse diet of bread, beans, goat cheese, and spaghetti, with little meat and only a scant ration of olive oil, fruit, and vegetables. For a recent five-year drought dried up most of the springs of the neighbouring mountains and deprived their few gardens and orchards of water. When a monk dies he is buried for a while in one of these gardens. When his grave is needed for another, he is dug up and his bones stored in a neighbouring charnel house. Here, arranged on shelves and neatly stacked around the walls, lie the skulls, hands, feet, and other earthly remains of generations of monks, whose superiors have boxes to themselves, with their names inscribed on plates or cards. The skeleton of one Stephen, hermit and porter, in priestly vestments, watches over them as he has done since the sixth century, and as in life he watched over pilgrims ascending the sacred mountain.

The mountain, rising sheer above the monastery, is Mount Moses, the Jebel Musa of the Arabs, the traditional Mount Sinai of the Bible, where God transmitted the Ten Commandments and other injunctions to Moses, to be relayed to the Israelites. Progenitors of the Jews of today, they awaited him, camped in their thousands on the sun-baked, shadow-splashed plain below, where the sloping rocks part to suggest a more distant horizon. Moses kept them waiting for so long that they thought him lost and, turning to their idols, gave Aaron their earrings and trinkets with which to make them a golden calf. This he cast for their worship in a cleft in a rock, now known as Aaron's Hill.

The ascent of Mount Moses is made by some three thousand steps, roughly cut from its face by the monks and maintained through the centuries. At the head of the last and steepest flight is the bare summit, where a solid pink granite chapel, with crosses cut in the stone, commemorates Moses himself and the divine interview, so fraught with moral significance for mankind in the ensuing millennia.

Tradition further insists that the mountain was also the site where Elijah, after fasting for forty days and forty nights, heard through a storm of thunder and lightning the still small voice of Jehovah. A whitewashed chapel, built over a cave where he is said to have lodged, before a cypress tree said to be five hundred years old, commemorates this solemn event. Chapels crown other peaks, notably the most majestic range of all, that of Jebel Katerina, to the naked summit of which St. Catherine was traditionally transported for burial. Her stone chapel stands here, with heavy stones to hold down the tiled roof lest the winds rip it away.

There is a splendid desolation in the panorama of mountains, Arabian and African, tumbling away from it to the twin divide of the Red Sea gulfs and beyond. Gleaming in the molten sunlight, they seem to have been thrown up from some chaotic upheaval in the bowels of the earth, then frozen in torment. Drained of all semblance of life, they seem to date from that moment at which God said, "Let there be light," and there was light and form but no living thing, vegetable or animal.

But now, in this far eastern corner of Egypt, the spark of human Christian life survives in the heart of a Moslem world.

REFERENCES

E. L. Butcher. *A Short History of the Church in Egypt*. 1897.
Robert Curzon. *Visits to Monasteries of the Levant*. 1897.
E. M. Forster. *Alexandria: A History and a Guide*. 1938.
E. R. Hardy. *Christian Egypt: Church and People*. 1952.
C. S. Jarvis. *Yesterday and Today in Sinai*. 1936.
J. Leroy. *Monks and Monasteries of the Near East*. 1963.
P. D. Scott-Moncrieff. *Paganism and Christianity in Egypt*. 1913.

PART 3 MEDIAEVAL EGYPT

Chapter 8
The Arab Conquest

When the Arab invasion eventually fell upon Egypt it was aimed at the fortress of Babylon and that crossing of the Nile which commanded the road to Alexandria, the capital. During the seven brief years which followed the death of Mohammed the Prophet, the Arabs, launching a war of expansion in the name of Islam, had swarmed northwards and eastwards from their desert peninsula to conquer most of Palestine, Syria, and Irak from the empires of Byzantium and Persia.

Now, in 639 A.D., their leader, Amr ibn al Aasi, was impatient to turn westwards and occupy Egypt. The Caliph Omar, Mohammed's successor, opposed this adventure for fear of a Greek attempt to reconquer Syria and returned to Medina to consult his advisers. Amr meanwhile went ahead with his plans, mobilizing a ragged force of some thirty-five hundred Bedouin horsemen armed with lances, bows, and swords, and pocketing, unopened, an urgent despatch from Medina until he had marched them safely across the Egyptian frontier. There he opened the despatch, which gave him orders to abandon the operation if he was still in Palestine, but to proceed with it if he was already on Egyptian soil. Thus, following the traditional coastal route of previous invaders, along the fringe of the desert where the Israelites had wandered after the failure of the Pharaohs to arrest their flight, he led his army towards the Delta of the Nile. Capturing, after a brief siege, the port of Pelusium, at its eastern mouth, he led his Arab horsemen southwestwards along the edge of the Delta to Babylon.

Here, since the fortress was strong enough to withstand a siege, he had to pause until reinforcements, led by a son of the Caliph and companions of the Prophet himself, reached him from Medina and Mecca. The Byzantine garrison was still stronger than the invading force. But its morale was undermined by widespread reports of the valour of the Arabs and their eagerness to die for Islam. In a spirit of fatalism the Greek Patriarch confessed to the fear that God had "sent these men to lay waste the world." Christianity moreover was split. Babylon harboured within its walls a strong "fifth column" of Copts, who saw slavery to the Moslems as perhaps no worse a fate than slavery to the Orthodox Greeks, and who had already helped from within to precipitate the fall of Pelusium.

In the end it was the Greeks who elected to launch the attack, sallying out of Babylon to confront the enemy who were drawn up before Heliopolis, with the desert behind them. After a head-on clash the Arabs, by superior tactics, encircled them and cut their army to pieces, driving its remnants back into Babylon and occupying the city of Misr before it. At a peace conference on Roda, then as now the "island of the Garden," in the Nile between Babylon and Memphis, the Greeks were offered alternative terms by the Arabs — acceptance of Islam and equal status with the conqueror, submission with payment of tribute and an inferior status, or a continuation of the war to a finish. Eventually they settled for the tribute and Babylon surrendered.

After a banquet to the Copts, many of whom were to adopt Islam rather than pay the tribute, Amr with his Arabs marched on Alexandria, a city at whose wealth he had marvelled during a visit in his youth. As his tent was about to be struck before departure, a dove was found nesting in it, and the tent, on his orders, was left behind as an Arab symbol of hospitality and protection to all living creatures in search of a refuge.

The siege of Alexandria was a hard task, because the Greeks had command of the sea. The Arabs moreover were soldiers trained only to fight in deserts, while the Greeks excelled in defence of the irrigated lands of a delta. Alexandria might thus have held out interminably. But following the death of the Byzantine Emperor Constantine, it capitulated by order from Constantinople, much to the indignation of its Greek inhabitants. Disregarding their protests, their government evacuated the city, the Egyptians were placed under Arab protection, the Jews were allowed to remain, the surviving Christian churches were spared, and a special messenger, despatched to Medina, announced to the Caliph, "Good news, O commander of the Faithful. God has conquered Alexandria for us."

Thus began the Arab occupation of Egypt, as a province of the Caliphate in Medina. To this day it is still a Moslem country. But from the start its inhabitants remained, as they were to remain through the centuries, predominantly Egyptian in race. The soldiery were forbidden to settle on the land, that they might be available for further military adventures. Thus they took wives and concubines from among the native Egyptians, including the Copts, and their Arab blood was quickly diluted. Otherwise the Arabs became socially a small and exclusive ruling class, adapting to their uses the existing system of government until, with the passage of time, they gave place to a ruling class which was predominantly Turkish.

Meanwhile, destroying the walls of Alexandria so that, in Amr's words, "men could go in at every side as to the house of a harlot," the Arabs built themselves a new capital on waste ground north of Babylon, in closer touch across the desert with Medina and still linked with the outside world through its port on the Nile. They called it Fustat, or "the Tent," for it covered the spot where Amr had left his tent to the nesting dove. Traces of it survive today beneath mountains of refuse on the southern outskirts of Cairo — dust-ridden underground ruins of houses with remains of bathrooms, oil-presses, granaries, and kilns, many of the walls still charred by the flames which were to consume it during the time of the Crusaders, after five hundred years of prosperous life.

Here, adjoining his own house, Amr built his Mosque of the Conquest, a primitive structure of mud-brick, with beams and columns of palm-trunks and a floor strewn with pebbles. Built on the plan of the Prophet's own house at Medina it was a place where his people gathered not only for prayer but for other public and ceremonial purposes. It was to be rebuilt and enlarged and embellished as the centuries passed.

Today its spacious, neglected courtyard is enclosed by colonnades with vaulted ceilings. Upholding them is a confusion of columns, fashioned from differing species of marble with capitals of varying styles, all taken, in the years that followed the conquest, from Byzantine churches and classical temples. Standing alone, within its dusty brick walls, in this forlorn, crumbling quarter of Old Cairo, with the desert at its gates and the rubbish mounds which bury Fustat close at hand, the Mosque of Amr has become an unkempt place, little frequented by worshippers. But it is built on a spot where the companions of the Prophet have stood, and thus has about it some of the atmosphere of early Islam, just as Babylon's neighbouring vaults, trodden by the Virgin and Child, retain that of early Christianity.

As the Arab Empire expanded and became torn by dissension among the heirs of the Prophet, the seat of the Caliphate, and thus of Egypt's parent government, shifted from Medina first to Damascus in Syria, under the Omayyad dynasty, and then, a century after the conquest, to Baghdad in Mesopotamia, under the Abbasids. It was from here, in the ninth century, that there came to Egypt the first of an intermittent series of notable rulers who have left their various marks on it. He was Ahmed Ibn Tulun, the son (or stepson) of a Turkish slave who had been sent as a gift to the Caliph by the governor of Bokhara and, taking advantage of a growing custom by which emancipated foreign slaves became preferred to the native Arabs for office, was able to rise to a responsible position at court.

Ibn Tulun, the son, an able and forceful young officer, well-educated in both the religious and the military lore of the Arabs, became governor of Egypt at the age of thirty-three. He at once reinforced his power and prestige with a strong and handsome body-guard of a hundred mounted slaves of his own, and soon, enriched, it was said, by several timely hauls of Pharaonic treasure, was ruling in state as an independent sovereign. He built himself a new and splendid seat of government, called el Katai or "The Wards," on a table of rock, chosen for its immunity to earthquakes, between the old capital of Fustat and the Mokattam Hills, that long bare ridge which dominates the Nile Valley from the fringe of the Eastern Desert.

Here, among markets and public buildings, was a sumptuous palace for himself and another for his womenfolk, with a polo-ground and a menagerie beside it, and around it gardens filled with scented flowers. These his son and eventual successor was further to adorn with an aviary of exotic birds, palm-trees set amid gilded tanks of water, flower-beds in the form of Arabic inscriptions, and a lake of quicksilver where, guarded by a tame lion, he liked to sleep on an air-bed moored by silken cords to silver columns.

Dominating all, Ibn Tulun built a great mosque which survives almost intact, no longer among palaces and gardens but above a labyrinth of streets, as one of the noblest creations of early Islamic architecture. He built it to replace the Mosque of Amr, which had become too small to contain, at the Friday prayer, the large congregation of his troops and civilian subjects.

As architect he employed a Christian, released for the purpose from a dungeon in which he was languishing. Unlike his predecessors, Ibn Tulun refused to raid Christian churches for columns with which to build his mosque. Hearing of this, runs the traditional legend, a Coptic prisoner wrote to the Prince, offering to build him a mosque with no columns, except two for the prayer-niche facing the direction of Mecca. On being summoned to the royal presence, he drew out on skins a design in which he replaced the columns by piers of brick. This his sovereign accepted with alacrity. But in fact such piers, new to Egypt, were already familiar enough in Samarra, a seat of the Caliphate on the Tigris, which was Ibn Tulun's city of origin, and his architect was more probably no Copt but a Mesopotamian Christian.

Within its austere double enclosure of high brick walls, inspired by that of the Semitic sanctuary as found by the Arabs in Syria, crowned with battlements of a refined Mesopotamian pattern, and pierced by simple rectangular doorways, the Mosque of Ibn Tulun gives the visitor an immediate sense of peace and relief from the hubbub of voices and traffic in the streets outside. Space and serenity reign in its great open courtyard, proportion and dignity in the arcades which enclose it. Springing from the massive brick piles are pointed arches, as seen at Samarra, but otherwise seldom before this time.

In its design the mosque has a monumental simplicity. In tune with it, flowing in intricate and symmetrical harmony around and under and above the arches, are bands of decoration in stucco, enlivening the architecture with an impression of continuous movement. Blending with them are the grilles of the windows, more static and severe but of inventive variety in their geometrical patterns, which frame the light of the sky in a delicate lacework of stone.

Spiralling up from the rooftop is a minaret of striking and unusual design. Cylindrical, on a solid rectangular base, it has an outside staircase winding around it. Legend relates that it was the accidental product of a gesture of Ibn Tulun, doodling casually with a piece of paper which he rolled around his finger in corkscrew form, then sent to his architect as a model for his minaret. In fact there was already one of similar shape at Samarra.

Illustrious as it was in its restoration of many of Egypt's former glories, the reign of Ibn Tulun and his dynasty lasted for little more than a generation, and Egypt fell once more under the rule of the Abbasid caliphs who had originally employed him. Within two centuries his mosque had fallen into disuse and decay. Used for a while as a camping-ground by North African pilgrims to Mecca, it was by the twelfth century virtually abandoned, found to be lit only by a single lamp and staffed by a *muezzin* who no longer troubled to mount the minaret to recite the call to prayer.

It was in its deserted arcades that, in the following century, a Sultan-to-be named Lagin took refuge from a murderous rival, vowing that if he were spared he would restore the mosque to its original shape. And this, on ascending the throne, he did at great cost, thus undoubtedly helping to preserve it for posterity in the form in which it survives today.

Adjoining one corner of the Ibn Tulun Mosque is the tomb of a fourteenth-century emir, Sarghatmish. Completed just before his assassination by the Sultan of his time, its slender minaret contrasts elegantly with Ibn Tulun's more formidable spiral tower.

Adjoining the other corner is the Bait el Kredlea, the House of the Cretan Woman. A seventeenth-century residence which fell into ruins, it was restored in the present century by an English Pasha, Major R. G. Gayer-Anderson, and on his death in 1942 it became a museum. Enriched by his personal collection of carpets, Arab furniture and woodwork, precious objects in porcelain, glass, and bronze, miniatures and other paintings and sculpture, Islamic and Christian, it otherwise typifies similar houses of this and later periods — those of Gamal ad Din, for example, and the Sheikh es Sihaimi — which still survive in the streets of Cairo. Characteristic of them all are quiet courtyards with octagonal marble fountains, cool, spacious rooms with decorative timbered ceilings, comfortable divans and window-seats and useful built-in cupboards, carved grilles to the windows to relieve the glare of the light outside, and in one at least a domed bath with fresh running water. Such were the cilivized amenities which came to grace a new city, built by the banks of the Nile in the third century following the Arab conquest of Egypt.

Chapter 9

The Foundation of Cairo

Behind Cairo's modern façade, with its skyscraping waterfront, refined garden suburbs, European-style boulevards and *rond-points* and opulent shop-fronted streets, there survives this great medieval city, which celebrates its thousandth anniversary in 1969. Within it there simmers and seethes a human life which has changed only slowly as the centuries passed and the modern city grew. A few main streets cut directly across it, as they have done since the earliest days. But behind and between them there strays without apparent direction a haphazard maze of wandering lanes and bazaars. Here fretted lattices lean gracefully out into the street from old brick houses. There concrete balconies, projecting from concrete walls, have replaced them. But everywhere, regardless of architectural period, there thrives uninhibited a human population of abundant vitality and unquenchable zest.

Essentially this is a capital close to the soil, the black soil of the Nile Valley. Its fruits abound — tomatoes, corn, sweet potatoes, oranges and melons, giant cabbages and diminutive limes piled high on the precarious barrows and stalls of the markets and street corners; pyramids of peasant bread with a pancake texture, fresh from the ovens of the bakeries; piles of fresh green animal fodder. For this is a city of animals, of horses, donkeys, mules; goats nibbling busily to right and to left; scavenging cats and slinking unclean dogs, like jackals; a monkey capering on the end of a chain at his master's bidding; predatory kites forever crying as they wheel above the rooftops in the hazy blue sky.

Horse-drawn peasant floats sway through the traffic, carrying a huddle, amidst their fresh produce, of squatting black-clad women and pajama-clad children. Sometimes the horse comes to an obstinate standstill in the midst of the tramlines, and a tram, full to bursting, gives the cart a push behind, to the ribald delight of the passengers. Mingling with the shrill cries of children at their street games are the streetcries of itinerant vendors, peddling bright-coloured sherbets from demijohns slung from their shoulders, or fresh water from skins strapped to their backs. Throughout the day there throbs through the city a rhythm of work, of industry thriving in a multiplicity of one-man smithies, in carpenters' workshops, at carpet-looms.

After dark the restless throng relaxes. The tumult dies. But life goes on. The shopsigns burst into neonlights, as though for carnival, in the flowing, rhythmical Arabic script. Bracelets of light ring the minarets and the loudspeakers of the *muezzin* call the crowds to prayer. Eating houses fill up, and at the street corners ambulant trolleys, glasshouses of gay design on wheels, dispense sweetmeats and meatballs and dishes of rice and spaghetti. Outdoor cinemas attract the crowds with Arabic films, and cafés blare forth Arabic radio programmes. It is late in the night before somnolence descends on the streets and the last prowler shuffles away to his lair.

Cairo was founded, in 969, by the dynasty of the Fatimids, who made it the centre of their Caliphate. It was a heretical dynasty. For schism tore Islam from its early days, as it has torn Christianity. It derived from the fact that the Prophet Mohammed had omitted to name his successor. Thus there arose two warring factions — on the one hand that of the Sunni, representing the principle of the popular choice, which had elected the first three Caliphs; on the other hand that of the Shi'a, representing the divine right in the person of Ali, the husband of Mohammed's daughter Fatima. Ali became the fourth Caliph but was assassinated, and his male descendants — those of the Prophet himself — were excluded from the succession. Since then the Moslem world has been divided between Sunni and Shi'a as bitterly as ever the Christian world between Copt and Orthodox, Protestant and Catholic.

Early in the tenth century a "Messiah" of the Shi'a in North Africa assumed the Caliphate, thus usurping the spiritual and temporal power of the Abbasids in Baghdad, to found the Fatimid dynasty. His empire soon extended westwards to the Atlantic Ocean

— a fact proved by the Greek general in command of its troops when he returned from a campaign with jars of live fish and seaweed to present to his master. Under his leadership the Fatimids then turned eastwards. After several abortive campaigns in which the waterless communications of the Western Desert defeated them — as they have defeated subsequent invaders — they finally conquered Egypt, their armies supplied by a fleet following the Mediterranean coastline.

Their first action was to found a new capital northeast of Fustat, on the road to Heliopolis, which they named el Kahira. Thus Cairo was born, and the Caliph marched into it in state, with the coffins of his ancestors who had died in North Africa preceding him. The name, meaning "martial" or "victorious," was chosen to propitiate the planet Mars, el Kahir, in the ascendant when the first sod was cut from the sand, unluckily in advance of the propitious instant recommended by the consultant astrologers.

The city was, in effect, a glorified palace — or rather, two palaces, eastern and western. It was built as a seat for the Caliph around a great *maydan*, or paradeground, with space for ten thousand soldiers. It comprised residences for his womenfolk, eunuchs, and slaves, barracks for the soldiers, and offices for his official entourage. It boasted among its other amenities a Golden Gate leading into a Golden Hall, where he sat upon a golden throne. Within a century the palace-city had grown to the point at which it was said to contain 4000 rooms.

In Cairo the Fatimid caliphs and their courts lived in sumptuous luxury, loading their women with jewels and manufacturing silks so fine that a whole robe could be passed through a finger-ring; breeding elephants and importing rare animals and birds; drinking wine and eating truffles to the music of song and stringed instruments.

Above all they stimulated the arts, employing Persian and other foreign architects to build for them, craftsmen to fashion them precious objects, artists to paint them pictures uninhibited by abstract Sunni conventions. These freely portrayed the human form as only the Shi'a — and especially the Persians — permitted. Education too was fostered by the foundation, immediately after that of the palace, of the Azhar, which was to develop into the great university mosque of Islam, and to spread its teaching throughout the Moslem world.

In the eleventh century a Persian traveller, visiting Cairo, wrote that from the distance it looked like a mountain, so high were its buildings, all whitened and cleaned by an annual coat of plaster and

whitewash. From nearby however its towering walls made the buildings within them invisible. These stone fortifications, with their
three imposing gateways, built by three Armenian brothers skilled in
Byzantine military architecture, enclosed the palace-city, and with
later extensions still enclose parts of the main medieval quarter of
Cairo today. With their formidable salients and bastions; the dark
vaulted stairways and chambers and passages, lit only by arrowslits,
built within their thickness; their broad *chemin de ronde* commanding
on the one hand the rooftops and minarets of the city and on the
other the desert, these walls survive, almost alone among the innumerable buildings of the Fatimids, as enduring monuments to
their architectural skill.

Incorporated in them, to the north of the city, are the minarets,
curiously topped as though by stone pepperpots, of a tenth-century
mosque, that of al Hakim. A mad, cruel Fatimid Caliph, with Puritanical leanings and "terrible blue eyes," he lived only by night and
made his subjects do the same, keeping women indoors by pro-
hibiting the manufacture of shoes for them. He met with a mysterious
end in the Mokattam Hills, on a midnight donkey ride, and is worshipped still by the Druses of the Lebanon as a Messiah of "divine
reason" who will one day return to earth.

His mosque is as spacious as Ibn Tulun's but in a sad state of ruin
and disrepair. In the course of its history it was misused as a prison
camp for the Crusaders, as a stable for Saladin's horses, and as a store
by Napoleon's troops, while today it harbours within its precincts a
modern Egyptian school. It looks out to the north upon an undula-
ting and now overgrown range of mounds of medieval refuse,
resourcefully thrown out at this point by the Caliph Hakim as a
barrage for his city against floods washing down with the rain from
the Mokattam Hills.

Adjoining it, piercing the walls, is the Gate of Victory, the Bab al
Futuh, a substantial and dignified entrance to the city, with arches
rounded beneath their battlements in a style which derives from
Byzantium. Over the neighbouring Bab en Nasr, the Gate of Succour,
more martial and severe in its design, is a curiosity in the form of a
heretical Shi'a inscription, which has survived defacement through
the eight subsequent centuries of Sunni orthodoxy.

Due south from the Gate of Victory runs a straight narrow street,
following the line of the old caravan road and the Fatimid "High
Street," and bisecting medieval Cairo as it once bisected the Fatimid
parade ground. The street passes throughout its length between

mosques and tombs and baths and houses of a medieval period, and through markets and bazaars still alive with its atmosphere, until it reaches the southern walls and the Bab Zuweyla, the grandest of the Fatimid gates. Its tall bastions are surmounted by the minarets of a fifteenth-century mosque, the al Mu'ayyad. The gate is called alternatively the Bab el Metwalli, after a saint who worked miracles by the door, so that the sick, in supplication, still fasten to it shreds of clothing and locks of hair. It was in the past a centre of executions, thus often adorned with human heads and hanging corpses — one of them the corpse of the last independent Sultan when the Turks occupied the country in the early sixteenth century.

Otherwise, few buildings of the Fatimid period survive. Today the flowering of its art can best be seen in the Museum of Islamic Art, on the outskirts of the medieval city. This museum spans the centuries from Tulunids and Fatimids to Ottoman Turks. Its numerous exhibits include architectural features and decorative objects from mosques and tombs and private houses. Here are marble mosaic floors, carved doors, hexagonal tables inlaid with ebony and ivory, brass and copper objects of all kinds — ewers, incense burners, pen boxes, Koran cases — with the patina of bronze, a variety of glazed pottery, and a large collection of enamelled glass lamps which once hung in profusion from the rafters of the mosques.

The art of the Fatimids is to be seen at its best in a collection of beams from their palaces, carved to form parts of a frieze, not with formal designs, but with scenes of everyday life, at court and in the home — and found incidentally turned to the wall of a mosque, their reverse sides used, to save timber, for carvings of a later period. Here, linked in their panels with floral scrolls, are dancing figures, lute-players, ladies on camels, servants pouring out wine, portrayed naturally and sensitively in a manner revealing the Persian and Mesopotamian influence to which the Fatimids responded.

Other Fatimid works, which have long since vanished, included, as a fifteenth-century historian has recorded, such exquisite objects as an image of a gazelle covered in pearls, jewelled birds, gold palm trees, their branches hanging with clusters of dates which were precious stones. Their tents were often made from silks and gold brocades, probably Persian or Byzantine, woven with designs of men, birds, and animals, and supported by poles of silver. One of them took fifty craftsmen nine years to make; another was named "the slayer" because several men were usually killed in the endeavour to pitch it.

Chapter 10

Saladin and his Citadel

The Fatimids were rulers given more to the arts of peace than to those of war. They were moreover heretics in the eyes of many powerful enemies in the Islamic world. Thus by the eleventh century their empire had dwindled, as an effective force, to little more than Egypt alone. A new and sterner power arose at this time in the East, in the shape of the orthodox Seljuk Turks, to reduce it still further. Finally, at the end of the eleventh century, there came a major incursion from the West — the First Crusade, whose Christian armies had soon overrun much of Syria and Palestine and were menacing Egypt. At this crucial moment the Islamic world threw up a great military leader in the person of Saladin, whose task it became to stem the Western tide of conquest.

Saladin was a Kurd, the son of an officer in the service of the Abbasid Caliph in Baghdad. When the conflict became a race for the Nile Valley between the Crusaders in Palestine and the Moslems in Syria, he found himself on the staff of his uncle, the commanding general on three successive expeditions into Egypt. During a series of confused campaigns in which the Fatimids supported the Crusaders against the Syrians — and in which, at a moment of crisis, the city of Fustat was burned to the ground to prevent it from sheltering the Christians — Saladin emerged as a military leader of genius and, on the final defeat of the Crusaders, became governor of Egypt on behalf of the Syrian monarch. He soon replaced the authority of the Fatimid by that of the Abbasid Caliph, but in fact came to rule over the country, with its people loyally behind him, as an independent

Cairo. The Coppersmiths' Bazaar, with the Mausoleum of Kala'un, the
Mosque of Nasir, and the Madrasa of Barkuk.

Cairo. Street scene, with the Mosque of Inan al Yusufy.

Ancient Giza. Sphinx and Pyramid.

A. F. Kersting

Modern Cairo. The Nile Hilton Hotel.

sovereign of devout and chivalrous character — "a great prince," as an Arab contemporary wrote of him, "whose appearance inspired at once respect and love, who was approachable, deeply intellectual, gracious, and noble in his thoughts."

Saladin was in Egypt for only eight years. The main task of his life was the defeat of the Crusaders and the restoration of the power of Islam beyond Egypt's frontiers, in Palestine and Syria. But Egypt was to become a seat of that power, with its glories restored and the city of Cairo built up into a great and permanent capital.

Saladin envisaged, in a grandiose town plan, the linking within a single great wall of the sites of all four previous capitals. This he did not live to realise. What he did, in fact, was to enlarge and consolidate the existing city by extending and completing the Fatimid walls, demolishing suburbs to make pleasure grounds outside the walls, and dominating all by the erection of a great military citadel, on a rocky spur of the Mokattam Hills where his predecessors had taken their pleasure in a "Dome of the Winds."

Inspired by the citadels of the cities of Syria, and indeed by the castles of the Crusaders themselves, conceived on the principle that if a city were captured a citadel within it could still continue resistance, Saladin's new stronghold was the focal point of a system of walled defences designed to make Cairo impregnable against any enemy. It became in effect a fortified town in itself, harbouring not only a military garrison but a civilian population, with its own residential quarters. Saladin himself, fighting abroad as he continually was, never saw it finished. His nephew and successor was the first to live in it; and thenceforward it was inhabited by the rulers of Egypt, almost continuously, until the early nineteenth century.

Its stone fortifications, springing as it were organically from the pitted, corrugated rock of the site, still dominate Cairo, looking across the great dust-laden monochrome city with its confusion of skyscraping monuments, ancient and modern, to the green strip of the Nile Valley beyond and the pyramids, monuments of an earlier millennium, silhouetted against the haze of the desert horizon. Many generations of rulers have altered its aspect, adding gates, towers, mosques, a "striped palace," a "Hall of Pillars" — and often supplanting as they did so the work of their predecessors. Today its substantial bastions are delicately crowned with the domes and pencilled minarets of a Turkish mosque, built in the Ottoman manner of Istanbul by Mohammed Ali, the nineteenth century sovereign of Egypt.

But Joseph's Well, penetrating nearly three hundred feet deep into the heart of the rock, is surely the well which Saladin's Christian prisoners helped to dig or at least to clear, and is justly named after him (for his full name was Yusuf Salah ed Din). Stretches of the ramparts survive from his time. Above all, the conception of the Citadel was essentially his, and this "Castle of the Mountain" still evokes the memory of this great Moslem warrior and saviour of Egypt.

To wander in the maze of Cairo's streets, with their dust and their litter and their pungent smells, is to come continuously upon buildings, medieval in date or in style — mosques, tombs, colleges, hospitals, baths, caravanserais, dwelling-houses, — which still play an integral part in the life of its people. The focal point of them is the collegiate Mosque of al Azhar, Islam's great university, now nearly a thousand years old, whose name means the "Blooming" or "Resplendent."

This too breathes some of the spirit of Saladin. Founded though it was by the Fatimids, it did not start to bloom with true resplendence until Saladin's time, when he made it a powerful centre for the counteraction of the Shi'a heresy and the renewed propagation of orthodox teachings. He reinforced this policy, whose purpose was as much political as religious, with the foundation, mainly for younger students, of similar but smaller colleges, both throughout Cairo and in Alexandria, on the lines of those already existing in Syria and Persia.

The Azhar has remained, throughout these thousand years, a living institution. Architecturally it has evolved and changed through the centuries, as successive rulers left their marks upon it. It has, for example, no fewer than five minarets in differing styles, one of them built with twin towers by a sixteenth-century Sultan, to overtop and emulate the more graceful single tower of a fifteenth-century predecessor. Restorations and additions and enlargements continued right up until the nineteenth century. The double gate of entry was built in the eighteenth, in decorative imitation of an earlier style, while the domed gateway which leads into the sanctuary beyond the great courtyard dates back to Fatimid times.

The walls of the Azhar comprise also a miniature mosque within a mosque, in the shape of an arched and domed fifteenth-century tomb of graceful design, where shafts of jewelled light penetrate through stained-glass windows; a library built in the late nineteenth century, which contains early Korans — together with a recent one, its 112 chapters inscribed microscopically on 16 pages by a calligrapher who afterwards went blind — and other valuable manuscripts; and quarters set aside as lodgings for the host of foreign students.

But for all the wide span of time which it covers, and its consequent confusion of buildings and architectural styles, the Azhar has a unity of atmosphere. There is harmony in its contrasting decorative motifs: in the severe geometrical patterns and the flowing arabesques of its plasterwork, like embroidery on stone; in the joinery and fretwork of its timbered screens, with the light shining through them. There is dignity in the infinite perspective of the columns, ten rows of them, which adorn its spacious sanctuary carpeted in a uniform red and swept clean with long branches of palm fronds. There is shimmering light in its serene open courtyard; and here, greatest of all unifying elements, is human life as it has been lived with continuity for a thousand years in the solemn study of the Moslem religion and the reverent worship of the one God.

Students from every corner of the Moslem world still throng this "campus," the arcades and the courtyards of the Azhar. Singly or in groups, sometimes huddled at the feet of sheikhs who instruct them in a curriculum only a trifle more modern than it used to be, they sit cross-legged on its carpets and paving stones, recline against its columns, crouch in the embrasures of its windows, pace to and fro in the shelter of its vaults, or sun themselves beneath the open sky, burying heads in the sacred books, swaying a little from side to side as they mutter the words, practising calligraphy in exercise books on their knees, neatly stacking shoes and turbans beside them as at intervals they hump their limbs in prayer or relax them in sleep.

The Azhar was among the last of the Cairo mosques to be built on a congregational scale, following the conqueror's original plan of an open place of assembly. The design was to change with the schools — or *madrasas* — which Saladin founded, following the proportions of the private house where the sheikh used to teach, with a smaller open courtyard and, as schoolrooms, two roofed bays, like transepts. This *madrasa* became the prototype of a new kind of mosque which survives everywhere throughout Cairo, but more often with four transepts than two, thus assuming the shape of a cross.

Such, conceived on a more massive scale than the rest, is the *madrasa* and mausoleum of Sultan Hasan, towering boldly above the

open square, once a polo ground of the Sultans, which spreads
away beneath the rock of the citadel. Flanking it is the Rifa'i
Mosque, a modern building of little architectural distinction but of
matching proportions, so that the road leading down into the city
between them seems to shrink to a narrow canyon between high
cliffs of masonry. The walls of Sultan Hasan soar upwards unadorned
and unbroken but for tall, shallow window recesses, to a height of
more than a hundred and twenty-five feet — and once rose relatively
higher, since the street level has risen with the centuries. Austere and
majestic, the building combines the strength of a fortress with the
grace of a work of art and the nobility of a creative ideal. On a moon-
lit night its domes and minarets — one of them said to be the highest
in existence — merge in silhouette with those of the neighbouring
mosques to inscribe above the rooftops an incomparable medieval
sky line.

The economy of its decoration is relieved by a grandiose portal.
Recessed between decorated panels of marble, it is crowned by a
shallow arch of stalactites, a pendentive ornament repeated around
the top of the walls in a cornice which projects from the roof line.
At one period of internal disturbances this porch was walled up and
all access to the building forbidden, since its strength and its strategic
position, confronting the Citadel, caused it to be used as a fortress by
rebels. Indeed the high narrow cavernous passage of entry suggests
that of some fortified stronghold.

It emerges dramatically into an open cruciform courtyard, brilliant-
ly sunlit and white, with a pavement of marble. This has four deep-
shadowed recesses, or transepts, each with a single broad pointed
arch leaping to the full height of the building. Here the religious
doctors of the various sects gave their lessons. Within the fourth is
the sanctuary, its walls surmounted by a frieze of Koranic calligraphy
interwoven with arabesques of a flowery pattern, and its prayer
niche flanked by two columns of a Gothic design which were taken,
with a third column in the porch, from Crusader churches in Palestine. Through a pair of bronze doors is the mausoleum of the Sultan,
handsomely panelled in marble, with carved pendentives of wood to
support its dome and, as a cornice, a wooden frieze of Koranic writing, so stylized and bold as to suggest abstract sculpture. The body
lies in a vault beneath a cenotaph of simple design.

This monumental building, at once mosque, tomb, and college,
dates from the fourteenth century, nearly two centuries later than
Saladin's time. Sultan Hasan had reigned — with an interruption

involving a spell of imprisonment — for ten years, and was executed just after his mausoleum was finished. He was a minor sovereign of a line of the full-blooded picaresque Mamluks, who displaced the Ayyubid dynasty of Saladin in 1250, to rule over Egypt for more than two and a half centuries.

Chapter 11
The Mamluks

It had long been the practice of the Abbasid caliphs to free selected foreign slaves, usually Turcomans, and employ them in preference to Arabs in the business of government. It was thus that Ibn Tulun had come, in the ninth century, to rule Egypt. They were reintroduced in the twelfth century by Saladin himself, not as administrators, like Ibn Tulun, but as soldiers, recruited to offset and reinforce the Arab and Egyptian levies and serve him as a reliable and well-trained personal army. After his death they grew in power, defeating, largely by the force of their own arms, the last invasion of the Crusaders, capturing and expelling St. Louis himself, and finally emerging, like Ibn Tulun and his successors, to become independent masters of Egypt. They were known as Mamluks, a name meaning originally "possessed".

What they established was, in effect, a long line of military dictatorships. The first Mamluks to rule were those of the Bahri, "The white slaves of the river," whose barracks stood by the Nile on the island of Roda, near the Nilometer built in the ninth century for measuring the height of the river, and still in existence today. As these officers consolidated their power, they acquired Mamluks of their own, private armies of loyal adherents who would fight to the death for their masters, and were rewarded with fiefs of land. Egypt thus became a country of feudal emirs, or barons, the most powerful of whom could become Sultan or put his own nominee on the throne, but always with the uneasy prospect of losing it, and his head in the process, to a rival faction which had meanwhile outstripped him in power.

It was a turbulent era that followed, in which conspiracy thrived and broke out into frequent rebellion, causing frightened merchants to close the bazaars and barricade themselves within the gates which divided the various quarters of Cairo, until the street fighting and the pillaging and the abduction of women and children were over and the current struggle for power was settled. Nevertheless, it was an era which threw up a number of outstanding rulers, and even one family which retained hereditary power for a century.

The Mamluks at their best were a ruling caste of abundant resource and vitality, with a talent for the exercise of power and, for all their brutality and barbarous practices, with a refinement of taste and a love for the arts, which they assiduously patronized, enriching Cairo with fine works of architecture in a profusion unequalled in Egypt since the days of the Ptolemies. They were also accomplished engineers, opening up the country with causeways and canals, roads, bridges and aqueducts.

The Cairo of the Mamluks was essentially that of the *Thousand and One Nights*, a "Renaissance" city of the Orient with a way of life virile and sensuous yet pious in its religious beliefs and observances. It was a city of drama and mystery, beauty and luxury, revelry and show, animated by a robust sense of enjoyment in which all classes shared. Its streets, always alive with dancers and jugglers and other street entertainers, were spread at festival time with rare carpets, hung with rich silks and satins, and brillaintly lit by night with torches.

A sophisticated court, with an intricate hierarchy of office-bearers, staged lavish processions and ceremonies, both religious and secular. The Sultan would ride in state upon a richly caparisoned horse, with a jewelled saddlecloth, the emblem of sovereignty, borne before him, a royal standard of silk and gold thread borne aloft and, carried above his head by a prince of the blood, a state parasol of yellow silk, gold-embroidered and surmounted with a golden cupola, on which there perched a golden bird. His court officials, richly robed and invested with the finely wrought insignia of their various offices, followed him, and a flute player preceded him, with singers and poets, to laud the triumphs of his dynasty.

Music played an integral part in Mamluk life, whether public or private. The Sultan himself had a band which at one time comprised four drums, forty kettledrums, four hautbois, and twenty trumpets. His more favoured noblemen were allowed bands of their own. Concerts were given on ceremonial occasions, in the Citadel, with a conductor gently waving a torch to and fro to keep time. Women sang to the nobility in sumptuous palaces and "pleasure domes," in a setting of fine carpets and hangings, behind doors inlaid with ivory, beneath carved and painted ceilings; wine flowed freely from goblets of silver and gold around tables strewn with sweet-scented flowers and laden with dishes of exquisite craftsmanship; incense burned in elaborate censers, and the guests perfumed their beards with civet and sprinkled their costumes with rose water.

The Mamluks, nonetheless, were a masculine breed, essentially warriors and, in times of peace, sportsmen and athletes. One Sultan, an Nasir, loved hunting and imported falcons and hawks for the purpose, granting valuable fiefs to his falconers. Another, Bibars, was an accomplished archer and a skilled maker of arrows, who, with the lords of his court, devoted much of his time to the sport on an archery ground beyond the Gate of Victory. But he was also an addict of horse racing and horse breeding, and spent two days a week playing polo. He shone as a lancer in tournaments, and was so good a swimmer that, according to legend, he once swam the Nile in full armour, dragging behind him an escort of noblemen seated on inflated carpets.

As befitted the soldier, he was also a thoroughly practical man. He organized an efficient postal service throughout his extensive dominions. For his couriers, relays of horses were kept permanently stabled at posting-houses, so that he might remain in continuous touch with all parts of the empire, receiving reports and transmitting orders twice each week. For more distant communications he established a pigeon post, keeping dovecots for the birds at the Citadel and at various stages. The royal pigeons had a distinguishing mark, and when one arrived at the Citadel, only the Sultan in person might detach its secret message; he gave instructions that he was to be disturbed for the purpose, regardless of whether he was sleeping or dining or bathing.

Bibars, the hero of the defeat and capture of St. Louis, was the first outstanding Sultan of the Mamluk regime. But strangely enough its first ruler had been a woman, Shagar ad Durr, widow of the Ayyubid Sultan who had died in that battle and whose dynasty the Mamluks found it politic at first to respect. A woman of strong character, she was the only female Moslem sovereign in history, and probably the only queen to rule over Moslems before Queen Victoria became Empress of India.

When the Abbasid Caliph refused to recognize her — had not
the Prophet himself said,"The people that make a woman their ruler
are past saving"? — the Mamluks married her off to one of their own
leaders, who was already her lover and who now, at her instigation,
divorced his wife. When he grew tired of her, Shagar ad Durr had
him murdered as he entered his bath. For this crime she was im-
prisoned in the Citadel, where she pounded her jewels in a mortar
lest any other woman should wear them. Then she was handed over
to the divorced wife, whose female slaves, on their mistress's orders,
beat her to death with their bath clogs and flung her half-naked body
over the Citadel wall to be devoured by dogs. Fragments of the
corpse were subsequently retrieved and given decent Moslem burial.

Not long afterwards General Bibars, clearing his way by a
judicious regicide, usurped the throne to become the virtual founder
of the Mamluk Empire. Abroad he emulated Saladin by a series of
successful campaigns against the Crusaders and the Mongols, the
new rising power from the East. At home he maintained a rule
which was strict and just, establishing an efficient and enduring
administration, winning the love of the people for his military
exploits, his charitable foundations and general concern for their
welfare. His main surviving monument, the Zahiriya Mosque,
stands outside Cairo's walls, at Abbassia. With its vast congregational
courtyard and encircling colonnades, its square towers at the corners
and its monumental gateway, it makes a fitting aftermath to the
architectural period when rulers still built on a broad and simple
scale.

Buildings of a different character survive from the succeeding
period of Sultan Kala'un. One of his sons reduced the formidable
Christian fortress of Acre and thus finally drove the Crusaders from
Syria, and his family contrived to retain power for just over a century.
Under these Mamluks of the late thirteenth and fourteenth centuries
came the flowering of Egypt's medieval architecture. They bequeath-
ed to Cairo a group of buildings subtle in design and more elaborate
in detail than those of the earlier age. They owe much to the influence
of the Crusaders, and incorporate into the Islamic style a harmonious
blend of Gothic and classical motifs.

Their façades make a street front, gracing that long narrow street
which links the city's two principal gateways, built right in the heart
of its congested bazaars where the air is thick with the scent of spices,
and the wares of the coppersmiths gleam through a spectral film of
dust. Here only the bazaar of the "Muski," the Mamluk Khan al

Khalil, with its opulent stalls and quietly strolling customers, provides a refuge from the bustle and noise of the traffic. Noblest among these buildings is the mausoleum of Kala'un himself, which faces the street beside the remains of his college and hospital.

Here, soaring to a high coffered ceiling, is a circle of great granite columns and rectangular piers, recalling the design of the Dome of the Rock in Jerusalem, but Islamic, not Byzantine, in character, with stalactite capitals and horseshoe arches. More completely Byzantine is the prayer niche, with its geometrical mosaic of marble and mother-of-pearl. The cenotaph stands in the centre within a fine wooden grille. Everywhere a richness of plasterwork, delicate as lace, and of woodwork minutely carved and inlaid, decorates the interior.

When the shutters are opened a white light pours in through the grilles from the pavement directly outside. But when they are closed, all is dark but for a kaleidoscope of filtering colour. High up in the walls, shafts and stiletto points and roundels of coloured light penetrate the lattices of stained-glass windows, at once relieving the darkness and enhancing its mystery, with a play upon the masonry of abstract patterns in glowing greens, yellows, and blues. Pervading the vaults of this tomb of Kala'un is some of the atmosphere of a great Gothic shrine.

The third of the great Mamluk sultans was an Nasir, a son of Kala'un by a Mongol princess, a small, strong-willed, puritanical despot, with a cataract in his eye and a cruel disposition. His principal mosque graces the Citadel, its severe walls relieved by the stalactite décor of its doorways, its broad unadorned courtyard by minarets of elaborate refinement, once covered with a mosaic of bright coloured tiles, of which traces remain. Such decoration, Persian in origin, is unfamiliar in Cairo except in the Mosque of Aqsunqur, the "Blue Mosque," to whose walls it was added as late as the seventeenth century. An Nasir's other mosque adjoins the tomb of his father, Kala'un, much ruined but for a Gothic doorway from the Crusader church of St. John at Acre.

Beyond it, through a tall porch of black and white marble, with doors of bronze inlaid with silver, a long narrow passage leads out into the hushed courtyard of the *madrasa* of Sultan Barkuk. Conceived on a small but harmonious scale, it has a sanctuary with arches supported by ancient Egyptian columns of porphyry, but otherwise Byzantine in decoration and feeling.

Barkuk was the first of a new line of Mamluks, no longer Turcoman but Circassian in origin, who seized power after a forty-year spell of mis-rule in which eight sons of an Nasir and four of his other descendants reigned successively but only for the briefest periods. The rule of the Circassians, based on no such hereditary principle, but rather on that of effective personal power and an electoral system, survived through the fifteenth century and into the sixteenth. It culminated in the enlightened reign of Sultan Kait Bey, which saw the last blossoming of Mamluk art.

Barkuk, Kait Bey, and other sultans of the Circassian line rest today with their courtiers and families in Cairo's "City of the Dead," interred in a group of tombs and mosques misnamed the "Tombs of the Caliphs." In Egypt, living and dead have always dwelt together in neighbourly harmony. They did so in the era of the Pharaohs. They did so even more in this great era of the Moslems, for whom the past was never far from the present and only a slender margin divided life from death, life on earth from life in heaven.

This City of the Dead, the Eastern Cemetery of Cairo, which spreads away northwards into the desert between the Mokattam Hills and those other hills of rubbish — thrown out from the walls of the city three hundred years earlier and composed largely of pots-herds — is today indeed a dead place. But once it merited the status of "city," with a large population which lived and thrived among the dead, looking after their tombs and mosques, running the con-vents and tenements and schools, and administering the substantial charitable trusts which the dead used to leave behind them. It had moreover a lively social life during the periods of mourning when families assembled, not only to pay their respects to the dead with prayers and Koranic readings, but to entertain the living, feasting and receiving fellow mourners in rooms set aside for the purpose in the various mortuary buildings.

Now, but for a haphazard village which crowds around the mos-que of Kait Bey, these monuments stand alone. For the living have forsaken the dead. The largest of them is the tomb-mosque of Barkuk built for him by a dutiful son on a grander scale than his mosque in the city, and once comprising in its complexity of buildings a school, a public fountain, a resthouse for pilgrims, and a "monastery" for *Sufis*, holy men seeking a place of retreat. Surrounded by the sands of the desert and built of its stones, the courtyard extends over a broad stretch of ground. In the centre, defiantly flourishing in the barren stony soil, is a single tamarisk tree, gnarled and tattered with age.

Characteristic of the art of these latter Mamluks was a talent for carving in stone. In this they surpassed their predecessors, who had excelled only in the media of plaster and wood. Here the two tomb-chambers, both of spacious proportions, are crowned by the first stone domes (with one minor exception) to be built in the city of Cairo, carved in forceful relief in a formal but vigorous chevron design. Replacing domes of brick and plaster, they are the fathers of other stone domes, covering the tombs of lesser lights in this Eastern Cemetery, which have been similarly carved in a variety of inventive abstract patterns. In the tomb of Barkuk, too, the pulpit, with which Kait Bey later embellished the sanctuary, has an intricate design familiar elsewhere in wood, but here sculpted and moulded as finely in stone.

This mastery, among the later Mamluks, of the technique of stone-carving infused a masculine strength into the more feminine grace of the earlier arabesque ornament. It brought to a fitting climax a period of fertility in the Islamic art of Egypt which had developed over six hundred years. It culminated in the reign of Kait Bey, the last of the great Mamluk warriors, who lived to the ripe age of eighty to become the most prolific and munificent of Egypt's royal architectural patrons. His familiar heraldic cartouche marks innumerable buildings of distinction, not only religious but secular, from his pilgrims' caravanserai behind the Azhar, with the delicate stone tracery of its façade, its row of shops of the period, its fountain for students and its drinking trough for cattle, to his mosque near that of Ibn Tulun, with its elaborate minaret, and above all this complex of mortuary buildings in the Eastern Cemetery.

In the design and construction of these various public works, Kait Bey employed architects and craftsmen of sophistication, taste, and inventive skill. They reached their peak in his mausoleum, which incorporates also a mosque and a school and adjoins other buildings — the tombs of his women, the ruins of a caravanserai and of a drinking trough similar to that at the Azhar — all once contained within a single walled enclosure.

Externally the mausoleum delights from all angles by the variety of its broken façades; by the balancing and piecing together of its component features — dome, minaret, porch, arcaded loggia, crenellated walls — into a varied architectural whole of impeccable proportions; by the sand-gold colour of its stone and inlaid decorations of a contrasting shade. The dome rises high, with the lightest of geometrical traceries, covering arabesque scrolls of a freer and leafier pattern, while the minaret towers above it, refined for all the richness of its ornamentation, and made slender by the tapering dimensions of the three chiselled balconies which encircle it like bracelets of stone.

Within, this shrine of Kait Bey is indeed the quintessence of Mamluk strength and grace. Everywhere, in the design and decoration of doorways, windows, cornices, walls, arches, and pavements, is perfection of detail in wood and in stone. All is deliberately conceived, delicately executed, and exquisitely finished. At the same time, no single part is allowed to detract from the whole. Transcending all is a grandiose design, bold and vigorous and voluminous, to which the the sum of the detail contributes. This emerges, by contrast with the scale of the courtyard and sanctuary, in the immense height of the tomb chamber, its walls soaring aloft to be lost in the dark recesses of the highest and narrowest of domes.

Here, in the tomb of Kait Bey, is the final consummation of Cairene art. Other periods have works to show, nobler in inspiration, more spontaneous in execution, more sensitive in atmosphere and subtler in feeling. What the Circassian Mamluks had to show was sheer accomplishment, aesthetic and technical. Conscious of itself, tending to grow oversophisticated, hence inclining to decadence, it proved to be the beginning of the end.

A new and all too powerful neighbour was emerging in the shape of the Ottoman Turks, who had occupied Constantinople not long before Kait Bey came to the throne. After his death and during internal disturbances which followed it, they began to show aggressive designs against the Egyptian Empire. These culminated in the reign of the warlike Ottoman Sultan, Selim I, who decided on its conquest. By superior military force and skill he soundly defeated the Mamluk army north of Aleppo and occupied Syria. A few months later, in January 1517, he marched in state into Cairo, hanged the last Mamluk Sultan at the Gate of Zuweyla, bore the last Abbasid Caliph away into captivity, and reduced the country to a mere province of the Ottoman Empire.

Thus ended for Egypt a long era of imperial power and glory.

REFERENCES

K. A. C. Creswell. *A Short Account of Early Muslim Architecture*. 1958.
Mrs. R. L. Devonshire. *Rambles in Cairo*. 1931.
Stanley Lane-Poole. *Cairo*. 1892.
— *A History of Egypt in the Middle Ages*. 1901.
Dorothea Russell. *Medieval Cairo*. 1962.

PART 4 MODERN EGYPT

Chapter 12
East Meets West

After some two-and-a-half centuries of relative obscurity as a province of the Turkish Empire, Egypt emerged once again into history at the end of the eighteenth century — this time as an element in the imperial designs of the West. Napoleon, already a power in Europe at the age of twenty-eight, began, as Alexander the Great had done, to indulge in dreams of Asiatic conquest. His invasion of England hung fire, so he secretly switched troops from the Channel to the Mediterranean, and embarked instead upon an invasion of Egypt, designed ultimately to strike at the British in India. It was his far-sighted plan to cut a canal through the isthmus of Suez, thus short-circuiting the English route round the Cape of Good Hope and establishing French power and influence throughout an area of increasing commercial and strategic importance.

Occupying Malta with ease, he proceded with his fleet to Alexandria, now a small forgotten seaport of a few thousand inhabitants, devoid of defences. On July 1, 1798, its governor reported, in great agitation, the arrival of French vessels "without beginning or end." Landing his men in a rough sea on desert beaches, Napoleon led them on foot over the sands into the city, which, after a brief bout of street fighting, was soon in his hands. The forty Frenchmen killed in the operation were interred at his command in the ancient Serapeum beneath Pompey's Pillar, where their names were solemnly inscribed on the walls.

The remnants of the Mamluks still ruled, in effect, over Egypt, no longer as independent masters but as governors for the Turkish

Sultan. Puffed up still with pride and delusions as to their own martial prowess, they were not afraid of these Frankish soldiers, scorning them as mere "donkey-boys," whom their forebears had routed in the Crusades and whom they would rout once again without trouble. In their isolation they were unaware that in the intervening five hundred years the ways of the infidel had changed.

It was a highly trained fighting machine armed with modern artillery which met and swiftly routed their medieval rabble of reckless but ill-equipped horsemen. Napoleon slaughtered them first by the Nile in his march through the Delta, and finally in the so-called Battle of the Pyramids, where he exhorted his troops, with his eye towards the monuments (some distance away, since the battle was fought nearer to the banks of the Nile) and a rhetorical injunction, "Soldiers, forty centuries are watching you." Thus Napoleon entered Cairo, with protestations of respect for Islam but maledictions upon the Mamluks, to be hailed by the "liberated" Egyptians as the "Great Sultan" — and soon afterwards to instruct them in the rights of man, fully arrayed in Moslem costume.

Meanwhile, however, the British were chasing him. Nelson and his fleet had in fact reached Alexandria before Napoleon, then had pursued him to Crete, where he was sheltering en route. But the two fleets had passed in the night in the channel without seeing one another. Now Nelson appeared once more off the Egyptian coast. Drawing a blank in Alexandria, he at last came upon his quarry at anchor in Aboukir Bay, at the end of the reef some fifteen miles to the east, where the French admiral had withdrawn his fleet for greater safety. Just south of Cape Zephyrium, so called by the Greeks for its cool zephyr breezes, the French ships were spaced apart in two lines behind a coastal fort of the reign of Kait Bey — still a military establishment today — and a fortified rock which was to be named, after the battle, Nelson Island.

The two fleets were roughly equal in strength, but the British proved superior in tactics, attacking the French not only from the east but from the west, between the fort and the island where they had thought no ship could pass. Thus caught between two fires, the French ships, almost without exception, were sunk or captured or otherwise put out of action. Their admiral was killed and his flagship, the *Orient*, captained by a Corsican named Casabianca, blew up, while his "boy stood on the burning deck, whence all but he had fled" — thus winning immortality from the pen of Mrs. Hemans. Such was the "Battle of the Nile," fought even farther from the river than the previous battle from the Pyramids, but close to the river's original Canopic mouth. It lost Napoleon the command of the sea and put an end to his dreams of an Asiatic empire.

"*Eh bien*," he remarked on receipt of the news a week later, "it will be necessary to remain in these countries, or to make a grand exit like the ancients." For the present, cut off from his own country, he chose to remain in Cairo, living luxuriously, with a French mistress, in the palace of a rich Mamluk named Elfi Bey. Situated in a country district, on the site where Shepheard's Hotel was later to arise, it stood by the banks of the Ezbekieh lake, the "Pool of Elephants," which was later to be drained and today, as the Ezbekieh Gardens, offers greenery and shade to the people of Cairo. Here Napoleon busied himself with the reorganization of the government, the replanning of the city with Parisian boulevards, the installation of marvellous windmills on the Mokattam foothills, the launching of a balloon into the skies, and a visit to Suez where he had reluctantly to accept the erroneous advice of his engineer that, owing to a difference in levels between the two seas, the project of a Suez Canal was impracticable.

Turning his attention to the Nile and to the Mamluks, who were still in effective control of its upper waters, Napoleon sent a force to Upper Egypt which, in an arduous running campaign up the river as far as Aswan, reduced them to partial submission. Thus encouraged, he embarked on an invasion of Syria and Palestine. But the British, with their command of the sea, held him at Acre and forced him into an ignominious retreat. The Turks, at British instigation then landed an army in Egypt in pursuit of him. But in a land battle of Aboukir he drove the army into the sea and destroyed it. This victory restored his prestige with the Egyptians, and the Mamluk chieftains were not long in submitting.

But for all his boasts to the contrary, there was clearly no chance of consolidating "this magnificent colony," and a serious crisis in Europe clinched his decision to abandon his army and return to France. Kléber was chosen to remain behind in command of the army — he was to be assassinated a year later in the palace by the Ezbekieh lake — and Napoleon sailed secretly, with a group of his officers and a Mamluk chieftain for exhibition in Paris, down the Nile to Alexandria and thence, evading the British fleet, along the North African coast and across, touching briefly his native Corsica, to France. Two years later, in 1801 a joint British and Turkish force landed in Alexandria, occupied Cairo, forced the

surrender of the demoralized French army and transported it back
to France.[1]

Little visible trace now remains of Napoleon's short-lived occupation of Egypt. He strengthened the medieval fortifications of
Cairo, adding bastions to the walls near the gates of the Bab an Nasr
and the Bab al Futuh, on which the names of his several lieutenants
survive, inscribed in nice Latin characters. He made a fortress of
the mosque of Sultan Bibars, beyond the walls, giving it, in honour
of one of the lieutenants, the name of Fort Sulkowski. A minaret of
the mosque of Sultan Hasan, beneath the Citadel, is studded with
cannon balls which are said to be Bonaparte's. Some of them may
date from the time of a revolt which he quelled by mounting his
artillery at the edge of the Mokattam Hills above, later decapitating
the rebels and exhibiting their heads to the crowd by the Ezbekieh
lake. The walls of the temples of Upper Egypt are carved here and
there with the signatures of Napoleon's soldiery — the first tourists,
no doubt, since the Romans — while within the gateway of the sun-
ken temple of Philae, beyond Aswan, his campaign is commemorated
by a grandiloquent inscription in French.

Nonetheless, the expedition made an outstanding contribution
to culture. Besides soldiers Napoleon took with him, under the
auspices of the Institut de France, a large team of savants. They included not only scientists and technologists but men of letters and
artists — historians, archaeologists, architects, draughtsmen — and
were well-equipped with both a laboratory of instruments and a
library of books. Their direct task was to study and survey every
aspect of this unfamiliar land and to introduce into it Western science
and culture, all under the auspices of an Institut d'Egypte, whose
meetings, in a Mamluk palace, were believed by the Egyptians to be
conclaves of alchemists, bent on the manufacture of gold. Zealously
they explored and recorded the pyramids, the Sphinx, Sakkara, and
with increasing excitement the temples of Upper Egypt, sketching
and measuring monuments, opening up tombs, tracing inscriptions.

One of the fruits of all this was the *Description d'Egypte*, a fully
illustrated encyclopaedia in twenty-four volumes, recording much
information forgotten since the days of the Romans, and serving
still as a standard work on the country and its history. These research-
es led to the foundation of the science of Egyptology, through the

[1] This was a prelude to negotiations for peace between Britain and France, which
resulted in the Treaty of Amiens.

deciphering by a French scholar, Champollion, of the hieroglyphics
on the Rosetta Stone. This trophy was captured by the French and
surrendered after the defeat to the British, to repose in the British
Museum — but only after impressions of its inscriptions had been
made, on Napoleon's instructions.

Politically, moreover, as economically and socially, Napoleon's
occupation of Egypt was profound in its indirect, long-term effects
on the country. It started a process by which the Egyptian destiny
became irrevocably involved with the Western powers and their
rival interests, at a time when the world was contracting and empires
expanding at each other's expense. Egypt henceforward was a factor
in the international scene.

Egypt's next and greatest nineteenth-century ruler, Mohammed Ali,
was an Albanian, springing from origins as humble as those of the
Corsican, from whom he learnt many lessons. Born in the same year
as Napoleon (and incidentally Wellington), in Macedonia (the home
of Alexander), then a province of the Ottoman Empire, he was or-
phaned in childhood and was brought up, nurturing fierce ambitions,
in the household of an uncle, the military commandant of Kavalla.
As a young soldier, serving with an Albanian detachment in the
Turkish Army, he was one of those driven into the sea at Aboukir in
1799 by Napoleon's army, but was saved by a gig of the British Navy.
Two years later he was marching to Cairo with the Anglo-Turkish
force that achieved its final defeat.

When the British withdrew from Egypt in 1803 they left a confusion behind them in which turbulent Mamluks and ineffectual
Turks reverted to internecine conflict. The young Mohammed Ali
meanwhile had built up a sizeable Albanian force of his own, and
with this he slyly supported now one side, now the other. Judging
his moment and seizing a chance to fill the political vacuum, he
executed a military *coup d'état*, capturing the Citadel with Mamluk
support, imprisoning the Turkish governor and, at the age of thirty-
seven, replacing him as Pasha of Egypt, with the final reluctant
agreement of Constantinople. He thus founded a dynasty, first of
viceroys and later of kings, which was to last until it was displaced
by another military *coup d'état* in 1952.

Internally, Mohammed Ali modernized the government of Egypt
as Napoleon had started to do, sweeping away dead traditions to
"arouse this land," as he put it, "from the sleep of ages." He welcomed foreign advisory technicians and traders. Economically, he

enriched the country by planting cotton and increasing the area of arable land. Socially, his reforms included the introduction into the doctors' profession of eunuchs, by whom women would consent to be medically examined.

Internationally, the story of his reign was that of the continued struggle for influence over Egypt between Britain and France. Two years after he came to power the British once again landed an army, with the intention of dethroning him and reinstating the Mamluks. He soundly defeated them on the beaches and rode in triumph through Cairo between rows of British heads impaled on stakes. Thenceforward he gave preferential support to the French — until some twenty-five years later when they joined with the British in the interests of the balance of power against Russia to check his invasion of Turkey through Syria.

Meanwhile he rid himself, once and for all, of the Mamluks. He invited all the adult male members of their corps of nobility to a reception in the Citadel, to which they rode in full dress, several hundred strong, with their retinues. After entertaining them hospitably he sent them home down a narrow rock-cut passage to a gate which had been locked against them, and here, where they were defenceless and their horses unable to turn, his soldiery ambushed and slaughtered them to a man. A sole survivor of the carnage was reputed to have leapt on his horse from the terrace, landing miraculously uninjured a hundred feet down. In fact it is probable that he never attended the reception at all, being ill in bed at the time. Mohammed Ali himself, hearing the hubbub of the massacre from his Council Chamber above, felt a trifle faint and sent for a glass of water. Thus, after five and a half centuries, did this dynasty of slaves finally vanish from eastern history.

Mohammed Ali's mosque and mausoleum now crowns this seat of power, soaring lightly over the battlements of the Citadel and the rooftops of Cairo below. Its bubblelike domes and slender, pencilled minarets derive from the Turkish mosques of Istanbul. Its architect was a Levantine Greek, and its rococo style and elaborate decorations in *trompe-l'oeil* reflect an age of growing European influence. Its chandeliers were a gift from the House of Savoy; its clock tower, designed in the Moorish manner, from King Louis Philippe.

The white alabaster which faces the building, however, was quarried in Upper Egypt. When a relative pointed out that it would be cheaper to import it from abroad, Mohammed Ali, the shrewd economist, replied, "When we buy in our own country its native products we are but taking the cash from our right-hand pocket to put it back into the left-hand pocket."

To contain his harem and to serve other purposes, Mohammed Ali built beyond the walls of the mosque the Bijou Palace, which is now a museum. An elegant example of the late Ottoman style, its rooms painted with murals in an Italianate *trompe-l'oeil* manner, it was the first of a number of palaces erected in and around Cairo and Alexandria, amid spacious gardens, throughout the nineteenth and early twentieth centuries by various members of his family of nearly a hundred descendants. Today several of them are museums, while some — notably the Manial on the island of Roda — are hotels.

The most prolific builder of palaces was Mohammed Ali's grandson, Ismail Pasha. To him the Sultan, in return for magnificent presents in cash and in kind, granted the hereditary viceregal title of Khedive — but not that of monarch, to which he aspired. He thus came to be treated by foreign rulers, including Queen Victoria, as a sovereign in his own right, and was granted royal honours on visits to Paris and London.

Besides palaces he built railways throughout the Delta, and westernized Cairo, with modern buildings and boulevards, aspiring to make of it a Paris of the East. The Suez Canal, fathered by Ferdinand de Lesseps and constructed by French engineers, confounding the calculations of those of Napoleon, was finally opened in the course of his reign. For this historic occasion he staged lavish festivities at which the guest of honour, among other European royalties, was the Empress Eugénie of France. In her honour he built, in the short space of three months, an opera house, elegantly French in its style, which still stands by the Ezbekieh Gardens. For this an opera on the Pharaonic theme of *Aida*, with a libretto based on a work of Mariette, the French Egyptologist, was written by Verdi. But the building was not finished in time for the occasion.

Despite the fact that a quarter of the land in the country was his personal property, Ismail's fabulous expenditure ran him into debt to the tune of millions of pounds each year. This was to cause his downfall. For it put him in the hands of the European banking houses, which finally made him bankrupt and caused the establishment of an Anglo-French commission of dual control over the country's finances. A little later Ismail was deposed and retired into exile, ending his days on the shores of the Bosporus.

Ismail and his successors made their headquarters no longer in the Citadel but in the immense and sombre Abdin Palace. Built during his reign in a ponderous Frenchified style and enclosed within high walls, it extends over a large area of the present centre of the city. This change of residence defied, with results unlucky for his dynasty, a prophecy of Mohammed Ali that "as long as my descendants occupy the Citadel their rule will be supreme."

Forebodings of this nature were all too soon fulfilled. Following a revolt in 1882 against the next Khedive, Tewfik, by Arabi, a young nationalist officer who seized the Abdin Palace, the British fleet bombarded Alexandria and British troops, after defeating him at Tel el Kebir, near the Suez Canal, marched to Cairo and themselves took possession of the Citadel. Here they were to remain for more than two generations. Egypt ceased to be a province of the Turkish Empire and became a protectorate under British occupation. In the political sense this lasted until 1922, when the country was granted its independence as a constitutional monarchy under King Fuad I — an independence sealed in practice by the Anglo-Egyptian treaty of 1936. In the military sense it lasted until 1954, when British troops were withdrawn. An attempt to reoccupy the country by a landing at Suez, two years later, resulted in failure. Meanwhile, in 1952, Fuad's son, King Faruk, the last ruler of the Mohammed Ali dynasty, was forced to abdicate and retire into exile in favour of the present regime of President Gamal Abdel Nasser.

The last of the royal palaces to be built — now a museum like the rest — was the summer palace of Montaza, occupying a stretch of the seashore amid pinewoods to the east of Alexandria. Its grounds embrace such amenities as a once royal railway station and harbour, a garage for three hundred cars, a dog-racing track, a Chinese pagoda, and an island formerly devoted to the exclusive purpose of drinking afternoon tea. Its extravagant rooms, ornate with marble and crystal and bright-coloured glass, contain relics of Faruk — his wardrobe of innumerable uniforms, growing ever larger in size, and, displayed in glass cases, such toys as cigars a foot long, miniature cameras and other intricate gadgets, gambling counters, a pair of silver handcuffs, a selection of salacious bedside books, and a whip with a silver-studded red morocco handle, designed for royal use in the bedchamber. It was in one of the innumerable sumptuous halls of the palace of Ras el Tin, built by Mohammed Ali on the harbour of Alexandria, that Faruk signed his instrument of abdication, thus concluding another epoch of Egyptian history.

Of the present regime the most notable monument, outclassing in size and in scope those of the Pharaohs, is the High Dam, an immense wall of masonry across the Nile above Aswan, which is destined to multiply the water supplies and the industrial power of Egypt. Nasser's government too has made its own architectural contribution, by the banks of the river, to the thousand-year-old city of Cairo.

Here is a skyscraping waterfront of gleaming white concrete, in which modern hotels predominate. It looks across to a modern tower loftier than any medieval minaret, rising above the gardens of the Gezira Island, where Ismail built one of his palaces and the British their racecourse and sporting club. On the upper banks of the Nile, at such cities of the Pharaohs as Luxor and Aswan, are similar modern hotels, built side by side with those of the nineteenth century, and accessible not only from the land and the air but from passenger boats plying up the river.

For tourism in Egypt derives from traditions a century old. Among the guests of de Lesseps at the opening of the Suez Canal was an Englishman named Thomas Cook. When the ceremonies were over the Khedive appointed Cook his agent for passenger traffic on the Nile. It was Cook's son who developed this traffic, acquiring the contract for the mails, refitting the government steamers, and choosing their captains so discriminately that one of them was dropped overboard for nearly running his ship aground. The healthy, sunny climate of Upper Egypt in winter was publicized abroad and grew popular. In the late seventies a hotel was built at Luxor for invalids, and very soon others followed.

Now both Upper and Lower Egypt are thronged annually, not only in winter but in summer, by visitors from all parts of the world. They come to enjoy the sun and the flow of the river which have created and preserved a unique land; to enjoy above all the monuments which man — Pharaonic, classical, early Christian, medieval, Turkish — has created within it over a span of civilization five thousand years long. Perhaps no other country in the world can show a history so varied and yet so continuous and so consistently rich in artistic achievement.

REFERENCES

Alan Moorehead. *The White Nile*. 1960.
John Pudney. *The Thomas Cook Story*. 1953.
Arthur Weigall. *History of Events in Egypt from 1798 to 1914*.

Index